THE
SOCRATIC
BOOGIE
CREATING CREATIVITY

By
Felix Bendann

Cover illustration by
Patrick R. O'Brien

 www.trafford.com

North America & international
toll-free: 1 888 232 4444 (USA & Canada)
fax: 812 355 4082

TABLE OF CONTENTS

PREFACE

The reader will find this an unusual book, both in its format and its content. The content is a full philosophy, however briefly sketched, and that is its main intent. This philosophy centers on the emotional aspects of our thinking. The center of this emotional thinking is creativity.

Because the philosophy concentrates much of its effort on creativity, a secondary but equally important content presents itself. A number of methods are presented that allow the reader to become intentionally creative. I am aware that the previous statement involves a certain heretical attitude towards contemporary beliefs. Those who have bypassed religion and find their spiritual fulfillment in the mystique of the arts and creativity hold firmly to the belief that only a few of us are significantly creative. These few are 'fortunate' or 'lucky' to be that way; they are recipients of a spiritual gift. To suggest that all of us are creative, and that there are methods available that allow all of us to create when and where we choose, is heretical. Yet the book contains just such methods, methods available for the most part to anyone from adolescence on. The book, then, is a philosophy that doubles as an instruction manual for intentional creativity.

If the preceding seems at this point difficult to assimilate, there is more. The reader will quickly become aware that, with the exception of the last chapter, the book is a series of dialogues between two people. Why? Of necessity. Dialogue plays a special part in philosophical thought and also in the methodology of creativity. The dialogues are at once an example of the book's main message and an explanation of that message. Secondarily, putting complex and abstruse thinking in the form of dialogue makes such thinking much more available to the reader who is not specifically oriented toward philosophy.

I am sure it will occur to some at this point that the book will have a somewhat diverse audience. It is written for philosophers and the philosophically articulate. It is written for artists and creators in every medium. It is a teaching manual for college professors as well as for middle and high school teachers, The diversity of this audience makes it apparent that not everyone will want to read the entire book. To this end, there immediately follows a reader's guide, one meant to assist the reader in choosing how to use and read the book in the most advantageous way.

On a kinder note, the book is most enjoyable and most readable. I hope it generates thousands of discussions between you and your peers, if for no other reason than that it presents you with a brand new way of approaching your life. Be advised: the book is a full-tilt boogie, so wear you dancing shoes....

GUIDE TO USAGE

Philosophers do not necessarily want to teach creativity or the creative arts. Teachers and curriculum planners interested in making students creative do not need to be philosophers. Artists would cherish methods for being intentionally creative, but may not want to teach and may not want to philosophize. Since the content of this book unavoidably addresses all these groups, I thought a reader's guide would be helpful.

The Socratic Boogie has ten chapters. The first four are philosophical and create the foundation for the a-rational mental process I am calling "creativity". Chapters five through nine make explicit the various methods used to access intentional creativity. Chapter ten is a re-reading of the major themes in the history of western philosophy; it connects the book to its historical origins.

A philosopher or one philosophically articulate will probably wish to read the book in its entirety. He may choose to start with Chapter ten or simply read the book front to back.

College teachers in English and the Creative Arts may wish to focus on Chapters five through nine, and choose not to wade through the first four chapters. If they nevertheless find that they wish to assimilate some of the background in Chapters one through four, the important conclusions in these chapters are printed in boldface type. One may then skim from conclusion to conclusion toward Chapter five.

Middle and high school teachers, as well as curriculum planners, might find it advantageous to go directly to Chapter nine. Chapter nine explicates an important method for teaching creativity to younger students. It also projects a vision of curricula change in pre-college schools. That the method cited in Chapter nine is also the most powerful method for the creator of any age is worth noting. Hopefully, reading the chapter will clear up this enigma.

The reader will also find parts of chapters five through nine printed in boldface type. The boldface type in these latter chapters is simply a teacher's aid; the boldface type stresses important aspects of the creative methods set forth there.

Should all of this seem unnecessarily complex, please remember that a great many seemingly incompatible truths come together in this book and find their true home. This of necessity creates a diverse audience, as the truths are applicable to a wide range of understanding and activity.

I wish the reader joy in his or her journey through *The Socratic Boogie*.

~ PRELUDE ~

THE NEW WORLD

Is not the world

Round?

Five hundred years after Columbus proved

That West becomes East

If you travel far enough,

Skeptics are still falling off the

Edges of their minds

Believing them to be

Flat,

And rational.

~ CHAPTER I ~

THE EMOTION OF THOUGHT

Anno: We've set ourselves a grand task. Thank God we are traveling in dialogue.

Domini: Yes. A novel paints, a philosophy marches, and poetry sings, all of them a monologue, a one-legged dance. Dialogue, now, dialogue is talk dancing.

A: Makes me wonder if dialogue can be serious enough for our purposes.

D: And Socrates wasn't serious? Every day, down to the Agora, making the words dance. You are equating 'serious' with 'control over the outcome'.

A: Dialogue keeps growing and expanding. It never really ends. It never goes where you think it is going.

D: You don't like the risk of transcending what you already know. If we just listen and talk, listen and talk, the dance is there. All we have to do is follow it to discover where it is going.

A: It may not wind up anywhere that matters. Don't get me wrong. I love to dialogue, but we need product. I need conclusions. I don't need to spend hours blowing in the wind.

D: Listen to the "I's". The point of dialogue is dialogue: sifting, listening, feeling, dancing. You know the controlling 'I' will gradually recede and disappear.

A: That is actually the part I like most: abandoning myself to the journey. We have, however, a serious task in front of us, a specific task, and if we dialogue, we won't even know where we are going until we get there.

D: Listen to yourself. If we are just going to rehash what we already know, we don't have to dialogue. To go beyond what we already know, there is a palpable risk. We must purposely lose control. We have to dance our way through a lot of difficult rhythms. It's dialogue or nothing. Do you want to analyze ourselves or do you want to boogie? Socrates is holding his breath.

A: Socrates can relax. I have been sitting here devaluing dialogue because it isn't strictly organized or formatted. The task we have set for ourselves simply cannot be rationally analyzed. It has to be danced. Are you ready?

D: I think we have already begun. In our world, there is a significant and powerful prejudice in favor of rational analytic expression. I can see the prejudice affects us. We have to deal with this prejudice and factor it out.

A: Agreed. I am apparently as vulnerable to the prejudice as everyone else in the contemporary world. I feel compelled to take the building blocks of definitions and build a great house of words that will last forever. I have been taught over and over that this is the only way to think.

D: I have the same background, despite my counterpoint about the joys of dialogue. And dialogue even uses reason, doesn't it? It uses whatever is applicable. So what is opposing what here? I can feel myself polarized: do it this way or do it that way, but not both. Never.

A: This is a fitting beginning to our dialogic journey. Why did I devalue dialogue in the midst of praising it?

D: Because any effort to think that incorporates as much emotion as dialogue must always be inferior to pure objective reasoning. There is the prejudice, but why is the prejudice?

A: The modern world embraces the rational in all things. The emotional is not rational. Voila: one prejudice.

D: Agreed. Go back to how polarized communication has become. What you read is either intentionally rational, analytic, and linear, point to point, or it is descriptive entertainment. And still, it is all a monologue.

A: The hardest part of dialogue is knowing what was said. On the plus side, dialogue mandates listening, reacting, and creating. It demands involvement. The reader must participate.

D: But that's the problem. People will tell you dialogue cannot be specific, that it just wanders.

A: It has to wander to become specific, but you are talking two different 'specifics'.

D: True. Are we being rational or emotional? Literary or analytic? And what does it matter?

A: It matters. You want the instructions for assembling your lawnmower to be linear, step by step, and direct. No listening for meaning. Put the pieces together, fuel up, and pull the cord. No dialogue.

D: OK. Monologue. One-sided. Instructions. Rational. No spaces in between words. No listening. And no meaning.

A: Sure there is meaning. Follow the instructions and mow the lawn. You cannot mow a lawn with poetry.

D: Granted, but poetry can change my life.

A: So can six-foot-high grass.

D: Then why can't we concede that there are two kinds of meaning, each valid in its own sphere?

A: I agree, but we will find in the whole history of communication that these two kinds of meaning always overlap each other, always seem mixed together. Which is which? And which is dominant?

D: 'Dominant'. These areas of meaning are in conflict. Should the rational replace the emotional? Does 'concise and clear' mean poetic or logical? The polarization I mentioned makes it seem as if only one kind of meaning will survive, that one kind of communication must replace the other. I personally just do not see the conflict.

A: You are not looking at the history of Western thought. Each succeeding century witnesses man making more rational links with the concrete world around him. Rules, systems, and logics resulted in science. Science changed the earth. Why shouldn't scientific reason replace art, religion, and all the other vagaries of thought?

D: But someone had to *create* all those new ideas. Not just 'discover' them through observation. That's naïve. The new ideas had to be *created*.

A: And creativity is not rational and never will be.

D: Right.

A: So why does everyone think creating something is a lucky accident? Or a capacity that some people have and others do not? We believe everyone can be rational. Why don't we believe everyone can be creative?

D: Because reason can be memorized and learned. Creativity is individual to each person and cannot be taught.

A: So we denigrate the creators for not being systematically rational.

D: Not really. But we think they are lucky. It is our way of putting them down as a class of people. How do you organize creativity? Schools do not have classes in creativity. They have classes in how to generalize, organize, analyze, and reason. Creators are envied and admired, but society sees them as somewhat lightweight. Reason is serious business. Creativity is a luxury.

A: Creativity is a luxury we cannot live without.

D: Don't tell the rationalists that. They believe they are within an ace of making creativity rational. Wouldn't that tie up a lot of emotional loose ends.

A: And I suppose emotions would become rational, too.

D: Sure. Psychology is a science, not a toy. Understand the biology of the brain well enough and we will not be at the mercy of our primitive emotions.

A: Look at the flow of our language, will you? Creativity and emotion are 'lucky' and 'primitive', part of the sub-mind. After a few rounds of dialogue we are becoming rationalists.

D: Yes, but we are also listening hard, so that will not happen.

A: So we remain suspended in the middle between the aural and visual, temporal and spatial, and emotional and rational. That is truly the history of philosophy. Where are we going?

D: We have to re-conceive the boundaries of these things. They seem to be in mortal combat, but they also effectively interact. **If everyone would stop regarding emotion as primitive or a hindrance to serious thinking we would at least have a start.**

A: That's a position in and of itself. I believe some human activity is primitive and possibly needs updating or replacing.

D: Don't get sidetracked by the rational bias. If something is rationally inexplicable, that does not make it primitive.

A: But the rational is, after all, responsible for the technological glory of the world we have today.

D: In which case art and religion are simply irrational holdovers from a more primitive humanity.

A: Something like that, yes.

D: Is creativity part of this primitivism?

A: Maybe creativity does not exist. There is probably a rational explanation for creativity we haven't discovered yet.

D: Why? Why? Why? Why can't there be two systems of human mentation, each independent of the other but wholly interactive with the other?

A: I think you have started on a new road. But what is systematic about emotion? Or creativity? Its lack of organization is frustrating. It must be primitive because it cannot be systematized.

D: Again, the rational prejudice. Reason evolved later, is more lucid, transforms the world, and is obviously the path to human success. Right?

A: Right! Oh. I was buying in. But reason is our only hope. What other direction is there?

D: That summarizes the dilemma: What other direction is there? If reason cannot save us, nothing can. Right?

A: Right. So why am I insisting on a dialogue? Let's just build a great Kantian critique and get on with it.

D: I think you were justified in backing the dialogue. It is the human creative vortex.

A: Oh, yeah. That is clarity itself.

D: Be patient. I am thinking that two important efforts are present here. We need to avoid the prejudice of rational supremacy, at least for the moment. It makes our dialogue travel in the fear that if it ain't rational, it ain't. The other effort involves following the Phenomenologists and then taking the lead, going where they have not yet arrived.

A: I don't even know where they went. Up in smoke, possibly.

D: Bear with me. Forget rational supremacy. What if the world as experienced emotionally, and what the mind does with that, is every bit as important as reason?

A: But the emotional sensory world is incoherent. Everyone knows that.

D: Let's assume it is not. Let's assume that the emotional world is inherently a-rational but systematic in some strange way.

A: If emotions were systematic, they would be rational.

D: Unless human cognition uses more than one system….and one of them is not rational.

A: Then you would not know it was a system.

D: No. We assume anything systematic is rational. I'm beginning to see where our road is going. We have made the wrong assumptions about cognition. **What if emotion is a more complex and sophisticated system than reason?** And dictates its own 'logic'?

A: OK. I see some daylight. The problem is whether we can talk our way through to an idea of emotion that allows us to think of it as systematic on its own terms, whatever they may be.

D: And systematic in an even more sophisticated way than reason.

A: Maybe it's an idea whose time has come.

D: What do you mean?

A: I was drifting over the history of philosophy. There seems to be a certain momentum heading in the direction you suggest.

D: Thinking seems to become more rational and analytic with each passing day.

A: Another assumption. Look more carefully. Reason is definitely in its ascendancy, but, as Heidegger notes, this begins to shine a stronger and stronger light on what is not rational.

D: Descartes, Kant, and Hegel—these giants seem to be the epitome of what is rational. And they help our case?

A: Yes. As reason grows, refines, and flourishes, take a look at what these very rational thinkers do with the part of their philosophy that is not rational. How do they use it or include it in their thought?

B: Well, briefly, Descartes moves the focus of philosophy from the object out there to the "I" who thinks. Kant goes further by limiting reason to the subject, and states we cannot know the real or noumenal world at all. Each thinker is shifting the emphasis from what we see to who does the seeing. Hegel has a temporal epistemology, unlike the other two. He puts reason in motion; this is why he calls mental process 'consciousness' instead of 'mind'. Even though all three place a great degree of weight on sensory intuition, they do not ever define it, except to think of it as a primitive stage of reason. Are you saying these kinds of changes are elisions or mistakes in their thinking?

A: No, simply that these shifts in emphasis from the object to the subject, from space to time, from quantity to quality, reveal an evolution in progress. I take these men seriously. I also do not think they realized that their thinking involved a massive evolution. As late as Heidegger, who favors the imagistic over the analytic in his writing, the evolution is still not clear. Philosophy keeps isolating and moving across to the emotional, without ever really acknowledging the fact. Even as it conquers reason, philosophy focuses on the a-rational more and more.

A: So something like phenomenology will become the philosophy of the future. A neo-Heideggerian approach.

D: No. My thinking here is that the light illuminating emotion gets brighter and brighter in spite of philosophical attempts to remain rational. All of these philosophers address the sensory or the emotional, because it is singularly important, but they will not address it directly or focus on it. Even Phenomenology with its focus on human experience refuses to take on emotion directly.

B: Wait! So a philosophy that heads toward the subjective, the temporal, the qualitative, the imagistic, and the concrete is really trying to handle emotion—without ever owning up to the fact.

A: Yes. You see it. Somewhere emotion, intuition, the mind as felt motion, for God's sake, must become the central thesis of some philosophy. It's been happening for centuries, since the Greeks. The more refined reason becomes, the less is it able to deal with motion and fluidity in cognition. The more apparent that fact becomes, that some part of our mental process will not stand still and be analyzed, the more important the nature of that motion/emotion becomes.

D: So one way of looking at the great minds in philosophy is to see that their concentration on the rational correspondingly emphasized what had to be discussed but could not be reasoned, namely, emotion.

A: They thought it was primitive; it is the same prejudice we had.

D: Phenomenology is still a mystery to me. It focuses on direct human experience as the origin of our thinking, but it doesn't deal with emotion directly. Phrases like "poetic thinking" (Heidegger) and the "body-mind" (Merleau-Ponty) are rich with sensory understanding, but they do not go far enough. Why don't they understand that when they discuss human cognition as felt quality, they are simply addressing emotion with a tuxedo on it?

A: If they spoke of emotion directly, they would lose credibility in the philosophical community. Emotion is irrational. Or a-rational, as we have said.

D: I suppose. And if you build a philosophy around the a-rational cognition we are calling emotion, and never refer to it directly, you are going to come up short; something will always remain inconclusive or unsatisfactory. Again and again they do not cross that magic line: emotional human experience is not rational, and cannot be made to be.

A: Maybe Heidegger and Merleau-Ponty did not know that emotion is the center.

D: And maybe they did, but because of their own pro-rational prejudice could not bring themselves to acknowledge or address it.

A: Pretty harsh judgment.

D: Agreed. A kinder statement would be that they knew where thinking had to go but didn't know how to get there.

A: Let's say this is true. Do we know how to get there?

D: All right. Let's see if we do. Let's make our own counter-assumption. **Let's say that emotion has all the subtlety, depth, and organization that reason has.** Let's start with that. It will keep our pro-rational prejudice at bay. And we have to look at very basic notions to get where we want to go. We can't afford to forget that we are entering a new kingdom with all its formidability and power.

A: Yes. I see that. We have to listen to what emotion actually is rather than what we have been taught.

D: So where do we start?

A: Reason is built on words, each word a brick, word by word, sentence by sentence, cohering as tightly as possible. What is emotion 'built' on?

D: Sensations, which are almost always multiple and discrete. All emotional experiences are clustered. You don't just love; you're also happy, excited, anticipatory, and a whole host of other feelings.

A: OK. Let's compare words and senses. Senses seem very specific, and their range singly and in combination is almost infinite. Hell, a wine taster can tell you within five miles in a region of France where the grapes were grown. How's that for accuracy?

D: I follow. We use ten to twenty thousand words to build our reason. If emotion specifically draws from senses, it has hundreds of thousands of discrete touches, smells, sounds, sights, and tastes to draw from.

A: And if this is truly a system, it has a much broader base and makes much finer distinctions than reason. So far so good. But reason constructs precise connectivity between the words it uses. That doesn't seem true of emotion.

D: Rational precision needs to be spatial and static, a brick on a brick on a brick. Within the world of reason, whatever connotes and has movement is a mistake, a threat to clarity. Is there then another kind of precision? Emotion makes precise and specific distinctions among sensations.

A: But we are speaking of the way emotion is organized, not how it acts. Is its organization precise?

D: Then the question is: How is it organized?

A: Its organization can't be architectural like reason. Emotion is always in motion, never a noun. We have to compare bricks to motions. The motion seems to be grouping and sorting by a same-different criterion that is very specific. Love feels like happiness, but each of those emotions moves differently, and moves differently enough for us to make a distinction.

D: But emotions never seem to occur singly but always in clusters around an experience, like butterflies around a flower. We are not able even to name all of them pertaining to a single event.

A: Agreed. Emotion is always in motion, and always occurs in groups attached to an experience. And we distinguish emotions by same/different comparisons. How can you organize motion?

D: Hmmm. 'Organized'. Not in space, out there, but in time. How is temporal motion organized? You know, our minds race back and forth in time at an incredible rate seeking emotional likenesses and differences.

A: So we can scan all kinds of emotional clusters in our past looking for similar emotions.

D: That's what I had in mind, but the question then is, is this systematic? Are these clusters of experience themselves organized?

A: I think only as linear experiences in time. We know when they occurred. This, which occurred ten years ago, is similar to this, which occurred yesterday. I can pull similar feelings out of my past by looking for them.

D: And somehow, gradually, these emotional comparisons reassemble experience.

FELIX BENDANN

A: Yes. Agreed. And these feelings are given names. Language is composed of a spectrum of movement. Emotional words remain moving. Rational words continually slow down the movement. Let's take a moving word like 'mother' and see how it is organized. Isn't 'mother' a cluster of emotions?

D: I see. Feelings have been drawn from all our past experience and given the name 'mother'. But you picked a noun image, a thing. Won't that handicap our inquiry?

A: I don't think so. Any word that is quickly alive for us is in motion and is felt. The more alive or present to us it is, the easier it is felt. Emotional words have a lot of psychic motion within them, regardless of whether they are nouns or verbs.

D: OK I see that. Reason needs the static dead words like 'inference', where emotion needs motion words. But 'mother' is a whole cluster of emotions and very complex.

A: And yet it is an identifiable whole, a cluster of feelings with a name.

D: Yes, but everyone doesn't *feel* the same way about 'mother'. Everyone organizes their feelings around this word differently. Their experience is different.

A: Granted. Each individual has different feelings surrounding 'mother', but that doesn't tell us how we organize those feelings so that we can use the word 'mother' between us.

D: Let's lay it out. Here's 'mother' with hundreds of associated feelings attached to it. But if I say 'mother' to you, we somehow share enough of those associations so the word means somewhat the same thing to you. How can that be possible?

A: The word we are after is 'priority'. Each image experience can have any number of associations, but there is a systematic shorthand at work. These associations are organized by priorities.

D: I like that, but there is a problem. What makes one association more important than another? Does each individual do this associating the same way?

A: I think so, but when you say 'the same way' you are also acknowledging that everyone's experience is different. Each person organizes different experience the same way, regardless of the fact that everyone's experience is different.

D: Which matters how?

A: Well, language creatures that we are, in order to use the word 'mother' intelligibly, you and I must have a number of those associations prioritized in the same order—but not all of them. No way.

D: Let me see what you are saying. Let's presume 'mother' has ten thousand associations, and most people have prioritized these associations so that six of the first ten most important associations are roughly the same for everyone.

A: Now you are there. The associations do not all need to be the same, just enough of them to communicate. Among my top ten for mother would be 'drunk'. Is that one of your top ten?

D: No, but I'll bet one of yours isn't 'died before I really knew her'.

A: Exactly. We all prioritize the feelings associated with 'mother' differently, but enough of the important ones are the same so that we can communicate.

D: That all seems terribly imprecise and inexact. We share a word partly and yet our sense of the word actually differs by hundreds of associations because our experience is individual and different.

A: Does it have to be precise? Maybe the system of emotions is not based on the kind of precision reason has.

D: **My God. You are talking about a system of approximation that actually works.** A system that starts with precise sensations and then purposely allows them to be imprecisely grouped into clusters of experience, only to go back, as the need arises, and compare and contrast a given emotion to get a more accurate sense of it! And it's a system that is constantly interweaving old and new associations and prioritizing them. **Just how accurate does a given emotion have to be?**

A: It depends on its importance in your experience. The more significant the experience, the more accurate it must become emotionally. There appears to be no absolute limit in this system, nor does there need to be.

D: And what makes an experience important is its presence to you, how painful or joyous, how dramatic, if you will.

A: Or maybe how often you encounter it. Images and feelings have different densities dependent on our experience. 'Mother' is dense for everyone. "Ice" is a dense image in the arctic, but perhaps not so much so in the tropics. I believe it is time to be more specific. What do you think when I mention the word 'ruby' to you?

D: I see where you are going. "Hardness', 'redness', 'precious', and 'permanence' are certainly among my top ten prioritized associations. Is it the same for you?

A: Yes, but here is my point. If you say 'ruby' to me, the first thing I think of is that my grandmother, who practically raised me, always wore a ruby ring on her little finger.

D: But then you are mis-associating. I would not know that 'my grandmother wore one' is what you meant by 'ruby'. Wait! That's not all you mean by 'ruby', is it?

A: No. I also include your top associations in my understanding. I have also learned, over time, that 'my grandmother wore one', although not incorrect, is not shared with most other people's associations with 'ruby'. At the same time I accept that my private association continues to have priority and stays with me year after year.

D: So your private association with 'ruby' is not wrong in any sense, but 'ruby' will always feel a little differently to you than me. And we can still use the word between us.

19

A: Yes. Communication between people also rearranges priorities of association, such that, however different our experience, we achieve an approximate common ground of meaning.

D: Well then, how about intra-self communication? Doesn't that re-prioritize associations too? Don't my internal experiences sometimes conflict and cause me to re-prioritize an emotion?

A: Now we are getting somewhere. In this whole mish-mash of clustered experience and emotion, there is a constant activity to group and re-group the felt sense of experience. The joy of the winter's first snow gets grouped with the joy of seeing your newborn child sleep or the joy you feel in the stillness of the forest. Despite the different experiential surround, we possess the sensory precision to locate the joy in each of these experiences, and we can prioritize these kinds of joy based on their sensory vivacity.

D: So emotion abstracts and groups from experience. Joy is multifaceted with reference to kinds of experience but remains the same, identifiable, because of this re-grouping. Emotion abstracts.

A: It abstracts in order to be specific.

D: But we just agreed that it is approximate in nature.

A: Both. Joy is abstracted out of each experience containing it and regrouped until our overall sense of joy is deeper, more multifaceted, AND more specific. A child doesn't just memorize the word 'joy'. She gets introduced to it in an experience and gradually accumulates more and more experience around it.

D: Some people do not even know what joy feels like. Rationally defining joy is not the same as experiencing it.

A: Each life is different in its experience, but the re-grouping, abstracting, and prioritization of feeling into images is the same. We all use the same system.

D: Oh. Right. Emotion as a system. OK. It approximates. It organizes loosely by 'feels like' and prioritizes images by 'feels most like'. It doesn't have to be exact. It organizes our experience as a sea of felt quality, a sea with words identifying the fish.

A: I like that analogy. **The sea is, like cognition, a medium where everything is always moving, always in flux, just like the emotional system.** New groups and new combinations appear all the time.

D: And there we sit on a big piece of coral holding our breath and observing it all.

A: Emphatically 'No'. You forgot. We never stop moving either. **We are the fish moving in an undulating swirling medium. Don't be rational.**

D: But I have to be. If we couldn't stop the motion and reassemble it by the rules, we would have no knowledge, no empirical science. We would be primitives.

A: I hear echoes. Is that you speaking or did a shadow move across your thinking?

D: Gotcha. The rationalist fear of losing control. The other system. The fear of change. The emotional mind is always moving. Always. If I embrace and live the motion, I can experience myself mutating and changing. If I stop the movement, it is to reason and control it. Emotion is 'out of control'.

A: That brings us to the tough question. If emotion cannot be controlled except by blocking it, what, in the last analysis, is its purpose or telos? Isn't it finally something that needs gradual replacement by reason?

D: Never. Pre-self-conscious sensory awareness acts before you even think. Without it, you would not even know when you were in danger. You'd be walking across the street and you'd note: "The car is about to hit me". Rational, yes, but stupid. Sensory awareness would have you diving for the sidewalk before you even self-consciously knew a car was coming. Emotion protects our lives.

A: You are crossing into another problem. 'The car is about to hit me" scenario is emotion thrust upon you to ensure your survival. "Emovere" in Latin means 'to move out'. It signifies feeling moving out. You are describing a reaction. Are both of these emotion?

D: No. I see. Experience thrusts us into situations where we involuntarily react with feeling. **When we are passive to the event and must react, we should call this 'feeling'. Emotion is definitely voluntary, something that goes out to have an experience or explore one.**

A: Yes, and there are all the combinations in between that are some of one and some of the other. At the very least, we can say that the ability

22

to react with feeling protects us from danger and pain. Enough said about this part of the emotional system. I am more interested in the voluntary aspect of feeling we are calling 'emotion'.

D: So why do we volunteer emotion? Why does it move out to something in our heads or something out there? Survival is not involved.

A: No, it isn't. Strikes me that there must be some invitation that provokes the outgoing movement of emotion.

D: Yes, some kind of attraction or promise of reward, but one not well defined or clearly seen.

A: So certain feelings called 'emotion' seek an expansion of themselves, which they do by moving out.

D: You know, we have discussed emotion in terms of its density but not in terms of its degree. 'Mother' is dense, but not invocative or evocative right now. I do not move towards it. If we want the emotion, we move towards it, or bring it to us. We presence it. It is a question of intensity. If we want more of it we go after it.

A: But at least on first encounter it doesn't need to be intense. What exactly is the invitation that keeps the emotion moving out toward something?

D: The emotion must be anticipating a reward, and not all emotion is a reward. The reward we are looking at must be a meaning or experience that is intensely pleasurable.

23

A: I agree. The promise of intensely pleasurable emotion would be a powerful invitation, and would create anticipation leading to further involvement. **Sometimes emotion can be immediately gratifying and voluntary. Sexuality comes to mind. I think, though, we are heading in a different direction, one in which we focus on emotion as an acceptance of an invitation involving a journey of some sort, a journey involving growing gratification.**

D: There could be many names for this. Plato called it 'beauty', the most powerful of all the emotions, the one guiding the rest. I like our notion of intense significance, something becoming more and more important as we seek it. **Perhaps, emotionally speaking, beauty is just that, intense significance achieved at the end of a journey.**

A: But many philosophers—Kant, for instance —have felt that beauty is also immediate. This has always bothered me.

D: I think this is a misconception, one arrived at when one thinks of beauty as a property of objects rather than a motion within the self. A Rembrandt painting is not automatically beautiful or significant. It takes a journey to see the significance and beauty.

A: Well, but what about, say, the Grand Canyon. Isn't it immediately dumbfounding?

D: Dumbfounding, perhaps awe-inspiring, but I maintain that if it is also beautiful and significant, the latter emotions will occur only after a journey. I agree, the invitation of the Grand Canyon is powerful and massive, and I might like awe as much as other emotions, but mostly because it leads me onward into it as for any other reason. For the canyon to be intensely significant, and not just dumbfounding, I must take a journey.

A: So be it. **We now have a movement out called 'emotion'. It moves out to accept an invitation to take a journey towards promised significance. If this voluntary journey ends in an intense enough significance, we call it beauty. So we have only two real divisions within emotion: reactive feeling used to guide our experience and help us survive, and emotion, which moves out toward the emotion of all emotions: the sense of beauty.**

D: You realize what we are now saying. After the survival response, the most important goal for emotion is to discover significance in the greatest possible degree. Is significance the same as 'meaning'?

A: Too big a word. Premature. 'Significance', in this context, simply means emotion smells something important in the direction it is going. I do not think the goal of emotion is as specific as meaning, which to me implies language elaboration. It simply seeks the important above all else. It knows 'important' because important is an emotion, or THE emotion.

D: So how much of cognition is this 'significance seeking'. I may be mistaken, but it seems to be going on all our waking hours.

A: Whenever we are self-consciously directing ourselves, we are mostly unaware of this emotional system at work. I would say we have another large discussion ahead concerning why this is so. Let's put this on hold for now and concentrate on emotion's goal. What makes anything significant?

D: OK. I'll assume this significance-seeking process is ongoing. What then is significance? Something important. What makes it important? If the significance is a reaction and involuntarily embraced, it is because it is a threat to survival. But voluntary significance? Voluntary significance must be about something hitherto unknown or not yet experienced, such that there is a risk factor, even if the only risk is temporary loss of rational control of the mind. But human beings also love risk. So one accepts the invitation and the risk to journey toward the important, or the promise of same. When or where does the journey end?

A: Good. I agree. I believe we have bumped into another rationalist bogeyman which has always actually functioned within the emotional system: intuition.

D: What? You are saying this journey toward significance or beauty is intuitional? Or is the result intuition?

A: Think about it. Intuition has traditionally been typified as sudden new understanding. That understanding was understood to be self-convicting, meaning true without being proven or needing to be proved. Rational philosophy has always denigrated this kind of cognition because it means 'true without further reasoning'. If intuition actually belongs to the emotional system, an intuition is the new discovery of something very important or significant. How it is significant is another story.

D: And reason won't accept this 'truth' because it is not rational. Reason would accept the significance after the meaning of the significance was understood by applying it to the empirical world, after the ramifications of the significance were spelled out. **Reason's position is that intuition cannot be true until it is verified. Emotion's position is that it is true because it is intensely significant.** They have separate goals and separate criteria.

A: Exactly. If you discover something important to you, it is senseless(literally) for me to tell you that it is untrue. You may not be immediately able to tell me HOW it is true, but you already know that you have discovered something important. No one can then turn this against you. How reason and emotion argue this out is another subject altogether.

D: But many times the intuition involves specific knowing. It is particular and concrete. That is why the 'eureka' or 'aha' happens. I don't jump up and down for the ominous looming 'about to happen'.

A: Be careful here. The exact nature of intuition is buried in traditional confusion. Whether you use the medieval definition of intuition as "a clear and certain percept" as Descartes did, or are simply referring to 'feminine intuition', these are muddy waters. We know that philosophy always accords intuition an important place in knowledge while never really dealing with it. Let's you and I simply accept the term as the culmination of the activity of the emotional system and go on. The exact nature of intuition pushes our discussion into the oldest and largest problem in philosophy: transcendence, how humans acquire new understanding. Let's take that on in another dialogue.

D: Yes. I don't want to stop our flow. **Let us just say that intuition is some kind of unity of emotional understanding, at once a process and the goal of that process.** We need to go back and determine whether we have established that emotion is systematic and methodical. Where were we?

A: I think we are in line with Phenomenology so far, although we are extending its conclusions. We said that there is in cognition a temporally interconnected flow of felt quality that represents all the experiential actions and interactions described by Merleau-Ponty's "Body-mind". We said that these felt qualities group and regroup across new experience, by a process of comparing the new and the old, the similar and the dissimilar.

We noted that this grouping and regrouping is approximate. There are no emotional simples like 'fear'. Each emotional cognate is a complex of other emotions as well, many times attached to the experiences in which it was discovered. It is apparent to me that the dynamics of re-arranging and re-grouping emotions are tremendously fast and tremendously complex.

D: Good. Complex because there is a natural shape-shifting taking place. 'Honesty' in one experience becomes 'rudeness' in another and 'embarrassment' in a third. The problem is not only linguistic but a primary component of feelings themselves. Since feelings are fluid and always in transition, and cognition itself is existentially always in motion, final resolutions are not only impossible but not required. **This is why we called emotion a system of ongoing approximation, very accurate as it performs, but never coming to a halt to be observed.**

A: Back to our water-world analogy. **The emotional system is about motion, experienced motion, which is inaccessible to reason.** Emotional motion may pause and its pause may be noted, but it never really stands still. At best we notice starts and endings when emotion redirects our awareness and attention. "Pay attention. This is now important. Let that go."

D: So we have a system of feeling which is constantly in motion. Feelings cluster around experience. Similar and dissimilar experiences are abstracted from their original locus on the time line and recombined. Emotion, like DNA, is a recombinant system. As these feelings regroup themselves, they eventually cross over into language and become images. Images are the names of feeling states. It is a shame that the word image is so visual. We need a word for feeling states which is omni-sensory to keep feelings from seeming static and spatial. Neither should the senses be referred to as nouns, since they always keep moving and function to observe movement. But we can't just coin new terms, can we?

Anyway, these images are comprised of associations past and present which have been prioritized according to experiential importance. This recombinant process is assumed to be ongoing without a break, and continues even in sleep. When we self-consciously become aware of this process and participate in it to a temporary conclusion, we term the process 'intuition'. The goal of the intuiting process was felt to be dual. It is defensive and protective in all reactive experiences. It helps us survive. Secondly, there is an equally powerful active phase of intuition involving emotion. We defined emotion as feeling moving out towards a goal. The goal towards which emotion moves was termed alternately 'beauty', 'intense significance', and simply 'importance'. We noted that significance properly meant importance and not truth. This sense of importance is initially pre-verbal, and initiates a journey toward maximizing the significance perceived. This journey and its climax we termed intuition. We decided to postpone a more thorough discussion of intuition. It is enough to state that this dynamic emotional system constantly brings before us new significance by employing recombinant imagistic cognates. **Simply put, emotion is a significance-creating system: that is its function.**

A: Nicely done. I think I need only to add something about the felt quality of something becoming significant for a person. We have been looking at this and now I wish to look within it. I want to return to the point when we were discussing intensity and degree of significance.

D: In the journey toward intuition, both the intensity and degree of the emotional movement continue to grow.

A: I want to bring back the word 'presencing'. I need the sense of presence considered as an action, a verb, in order to emphasize how significance is experienced. The journey has a reward we called 'beauty'. In designating beauty as the 'emotion of emotions', the prime mover, if you will, I feel I need a stronger linkage between our terms 'significant' and 'beautiful'.

D: We have described emotion as feeling moving out to achieve a higher degree of whatever was felt in the initial invitation. Can you link that 'higher degree' to presencing?

A: As experienced, yes. One notices something, begins to focus in on it, and as time passes the object of the focus has begun to fill one's consciousness. The moving feeling becomes more present. Since we are contributing to this movement, I say we are doing the presencing. The more present something is, the more 'in your face' it is. **Emotion moves toward its climax by presencing in greater and greater degrees until the journey ends.** Some journeys have a greater potential to be presenced than others, such that one can reach a point where the presencing is so intense that no other interest can be presenced.

D: And we described this filling of consciousness by presencing as extremely pleasurable.

A: Yes. At some point this presencing goes over the top into an intuition which more than likely occupies the whole of the mind. What was becoming significant has suddenly become intensely significant and important. A new aspect of the self has been revealed to the self.

D: And whether the invitation came from a work of art or something in the environment is immaterial. Something triggered this journey toward intense presencing.

A: Yes. And I want to use this language to change beauty from a noun state-of –being into degrees of a quality: more or less beautiful. I want it to describe the ongoing and frequently experienced intuitions we all have. Perhaps the word 'beauty' should be reserved for only the most intense experiences, but I would rather conceive the beautiful as experienced by degrees. **When something has become intense, has presenced itself to the point of real significance, it is beautiful and** becoming more so. This activity, past survival, is the primal and most powerful emotion in the human sensorium.

D: So. It is voluntary. It is intense. This intensity involves a high degree of presencing. The beautiful is then a degree of voluntary intense presencing often culminating in an intuition.

A: That's about what I wanted to add. I am not sure at this point whether the intuition indicates that the experience has reached a certain *degree* of presence or significance that evokes the word 'beautiful' or whether intuition actually signals a change in the *kind* of experience, a going over the top, which evokes the word 'beautiful'. We'll have to talk this later. At least we seem to have a good handle on the shape of the emotional system.

D: Unfortunately, riding along inside the emotional system for as long as we have has created another serious problem for me. Do you see it?

A: I think I do. My sense of the shape of the mind and mental processing has evolved to such a degree that Freudian descriptions of the 'mind' seem as outdated as the horse and buggy.

D: We need a dialogue on the shape of the mind and its structure.

A: We'll take that on next, if you like. First, I think we had better make sure that dialogue will continue to be the best vehicle to use for discussion.

D: More than ever, except for one thing. Is the dialogue within my mind really a dialogue?

A: That is critical for the next discussion, isn't it?

D: It is a very interior problem, and a very primary one. Chat me up.

A: When you speak within your mind, do you speak as if you were speaking to a wall or do you speak as if someone were listening?

D: What? I don't recite to myself, if that is what you mean. Oh. I see. I **always speak to myself as if someone were listening.** How do I know this? Everyone knows this intuitively, I suppose. I certainly was not taught to do this. Wait! Is the self plural? You opened a large can of worms.

A: No need to panic. Maybe we'll come back to this later. **It is enough to know that we can absolutely state that when we speak within our minds, we are being listened to.** Who listens is not important now. **What is important is that our intra-mind speech is already a dialogue.** Our permission to continue dialoguing is now backed by the awareness that dialogue is natural within the mind. It must be effective in ways we have not even touched upon.

D: Good old Socrates. I knew he would not let us down. Onward!

A: Don't you wonder what it is that we have been talking about all this time? We never even used the word.

D: That's why I am not 'wondering'. The word is 'creativity'.

A: So why can't we use this emotional intuitive activity more effectively? It is a remarkable system. Why can't we be more creative?

D: If we could become more creative, all the doors to the self would open.

A: That is what we are really talking about, isn't it?

D: In the last analysis, yes. Which is when we will probably get to it. Because, as you and I should know by now...

A & D: That's another dialogue.

~ CHAPTER II ~

Moveo Ergo Sum

Anno: Seeing the organization and power of the emotional system helps me regard reason and emotion as equals, but unfortunately it does little to clarify the shape of mental processing.

Domini: I do not think we are ready to reach for the shape of the mind yet, although that is what we intended in this dialogue. There is something stopping us, and we should deal with it now.

A: Discussing emotion gave me a better sense of the fish that we also are, the fish moving in a moving emotional sea, but I still want to stand on land and look for a static spatial structure like 'Being'.

D: That's my problem. Old habits die hard. We need a far better sense of kinetic organization, a sense of the way motion organizes within itself without reference to nouns. And I need to experience this, not just observe it.

A: We still want to use the rational tools. Our central problem is about cognitive motion. Reason cannot address this. We feel ourselves in constant motion. Why can't we talk it?

D: We must stop looking at it from the outside. We must be the fish. I know one thing that stops us.

A: The structure of the language we use.

D: What is true of German, Greek, and all the Romance languages? They are all subject –object noun-dominant languages. 'The man crossed the road'. Some thing, some noun, moves and affects something else. Motion is always a property of and predicated of the thing. It forces us to regard human beings as primarily things.

A: That is self-defeating. We cannot arbitrarily change language syntax to suit our purposes, regardless of whether human beings are primarily verbs and secondarily things.

D: Agreed, but look at the existing impediment our syntax represents. I want to speak about emotion, something that originates in movement and is not a thing. I need verb sentences. I need to verb-alize syntax. I need to convey the idea that motion begets motion and speak from within that understanding. How can I do this when language forces me to begin with the *thing*?

A: Heidegger tried that, but his writing is very idiosyncratic and difficult to read. He verb-alized everything and broke syntax into new pieces.

D: And I did get a better sense of cognitive motion because of the way he used language. I felt it as much as I comprehended it, but I do not think we can dialogue like that. It is true that the later Heidegger turned to dialogues, and these are intriguing, but they are also Eastern and enigmatic. If you and I are going to get anywhere, it will be by using the everyday language of plain speech. I am not up to a Zen conversation full of riddles.

A: We can do one thing Heidegger did, and Nietzsche before him. We can use highly connotative language and think with it. Heidegger and Nietzsche proved that. Connotative language is expansive, full of image and movement. It is vivid and full of speed. That is essential if we are to inject a sense of motion into our thinking.

D: Less analytical and more descriptively expansive. I like that, but I still want to ask if we really believe in the organized power of cognitive motion. I am 'floundering' in my sea trying to locate myself.

A: Let's stand outside and look in for a bit. We generally experience cognitive motion as everyday awareness of being awake and alive. On the other hand we have noted that there is great speed involved in pro- cessing sensation in a rather short space of time. Something is not right in our perception.

D: Let me understand you correctly. If you could feel the great speed involved in emotional processing, you would be more convinced of its sophistication and power?

A: Yes. The bias is that self-conscious rational thought is quick, while the emotional evolution within experience is slow. I know emotion can be singularly sudden, but I do not mean 'quick' in that sense. Emotion as a process of change is slow: that is the prejudice. If I knew this was actually a fast powerful process, I would regard it differently. I am all too familiar with the speed of reason.

D: I can start us off. I need one neologism to begin, the word 'interphasic'. As the emotional mind travels back and forth in time, it does not move ponderously from place to place but quickly from sensation to sensation. It moves, in effect, from motion to motion. I want to call this quick travel 'interphasic'.

A: Can you give me an example?

D: I was reading a novel this morning and it suddenly occurred to me to pick a page and count the number of times the author changed time tenses on that page. I moved from verb to verb and added it up.

A: So he changed tenses three or four times. So what?

D: He changed tenses over twenty-five times on that page. I looked at other pages and the changes were never under twenty.

A: I would never have guessed. And this was normal writing! How facilely and quickly we move back and forth in time without even being aware of it. And I have to assume that the emotional thought processes of the author were moving a great deal faster than the written words.

D: Does that give you a better sense of emotional speed, speed we all but take for granted?

A: Absolutely. My problem over and over is thinking that emotion must travel in language and that there are so many dead words, denotative abstract unmoving words, that emotion is continually brought to a halt by them. **The truth is that emotional processing is not a word-based activity but one based on non-verbal sensation.**

D: Such that feeling is moving through sensation that is itself always kinetic to begin with. The smallest parts of emotion are non-linguistic felt movements, and these are unimpeded by words.

A: And since this feeling is not linguistic, it moves faster than thought could ever track or comprehend.

D: Which is why it cannot be <u>reasoned</u> in words. Did you ever read a book titled *The Spell of the Sensuous* by David Abram? He postulates that the emotional mind is much like what we assume primitive man used. A mind that was primarily animistic.

A: You mean when language was just beginning to evolve and the stones and the wind and the trees had names? How does that help us?

D: It does if you take a closer look than that. Animism really means a sense that everything is in motion and by virtue of being in motion is therefore alive. Nothing in such a world is inert. Either it is moving or I am moving. If I stub my toe on a rock, did the rock move or did I? Causality did not govern that early world. Everything was assumed to be a distinct kind of motion and all these motions were interconnected.

A: I am starting to see, but these people were, after all, primitives. They had little language and less science. Of course the whole of their experience was in motion and alive.

D: These people were experiencing the world animistically. The emotional mind was dominant. Neither language nor reason was there to impede their sense that the world was in motion. They lived in a world of pure motion.

A: They are our fish! Moving in a moving world, a world where all movements are related. Emotion was their world. But they were primitives.

D: Abram states at the end of his book that he had tried to give an animistic account of reason instead of a rational account of animism. I like his thrust. He shows you what the emotional world would be like for human life if emotion was dominant.

A: A world where everything is alive and felt and moving. Hmmm. So these were human minds charged with emotion, ones with a sense that everything moves. Movement first, thinghood second. A world where everything is constantly presencing and changing. An electric world by comparison to ours.

D: Exactly. The experienced world without language and reason to dominate it. Not primitive necessarily, but a world where feeling dominated the whole mind. For us this happens only infrequently.

A: Then this is partly what we are looking for, a world where this cognitive motion held sway, where the emotional system was dominant. This is human life run by a completely different system than we use. It is the same sophisticated emotional system we have been discussing. Rocks pushing on trees, lightning rearranging the landscape, wind beginning as a caress and building up to a powerful fist. I can feel it. These people did a great deal of listening and feeling.

D: And they didn't need our powerful sense of the 'I' to do it. Who moved? Something. Was it them, the world, the inside voice, or the outside life? No matter. It was all alive and felt to be one, including the person experiencing it.

A: This helps me. It's not about speed of emotion but emotion dominating one's world. I have experienced this. When I go stand in a forest I simply shut down and listen to my world. I become non-verbal and animistic. Emotion dominates. Reason disappears for a while. Everything begins to move and relate and communicate. OK. Now I can feel the emotional mind. This is a separate mind altogether: the a-rational emotional system.

D: I suggest there is even more to this than the animistic experience. However lovely it is, the animistic experience does not convince you of the systematic power of the emotional system, does it?

A: Not really. I enjoy it and see it as a separate phenomenon, but emotion cannot solve the difficult tasks in mental processing. That's left to reason.

D: Let me introduce something here. Do you know that vision can distinguish between seven million shades of color?

A: Incredible!

D: And even if the other senses have not developed this level of discrete perception, you are talking about sense perceptions which have a range of distinctions among the tens of millions. And these distinctions are somehow coordinated and assessed among five asymmetrically constructed senses. And all this data is summarized and given to you every waking moment of your life.

A: I yield. This system could never be rationally self-conscious. I wouldn't begin to know how to operate something as complex as this. I need some kind of analogy to even conceive of it.

D: Let's add up what we know about this system. Maybe it just hasn't come together yet. Emotional associations occur at great speed within cognition. This interphasic associative process is extremely complex as it draws from all the millions of particular sensations reported by the five senses. It constantly processes our experience in time, arranging the felt patterns and configurations into comprehensible moving wholes that orient us in the world. At any given point it provides us with a sense of who we are, when and where we are, and what to pay attention to. In effect, it delivers us to ourselves at any given moment. We don't operate this system. It operates itself and is simply there for us.

A: The Idiot-Savant.

D: Come on in from left field. Where are you?

A: An Idiot-Savant is the fellow who takes about five seconds to tell you that May 14, 1503 occurred on a Saturday. He is the fellow who hears a symphony and can sit down and play it on piano. Yet you don't send him to the store for a loaf of bread because he might get disoriented and lose his way.

D: Yes? So? He is a marvelous freak. So what?

A: Don't you see? Where does he malfunction? Experientially. Nothing is putting his felt experience together for him. Yet he can access within himself what I would have to call a computer.

D: Yes, his computer works much like the ones we now construct. It's mathematical and fast at computations. If we all have such a computer, the Idiot-Savant is the only type of human who can access it. So?

A: Put it together! What makes him such an anomaly is that his computational processing is separated from his sensations. He doesn't possess what you and I take for granted, experiential moment to moment orientation in time and space.

D: That was quite a leap. You are claiming that human beings possess a working computer but the basis of its computation is emotion? Sensation?

A: Yes. Nothing can explain the speed with which we process experience, given its sensate complexity. We aren't even conscious of doing it. It is distinctly not the case that humans sense selectively or do not sense much of what takes place. We have to sense everything changing around us. Our survival is dependent on that, just like the survival of the fish depends on constant orientation in a moving changing environment. We have an animistic computer.

D: Why a computer? We process sensation, link it together, and sort it out and store it.

A: Millions of sensations, the input of five qualitatively different sense reportings. Without an emotional computer it would take us ten years to walk across the room.

D: So somehow sensation is prioritized and organized to create experiential order, an order derived from thousands of inputs a minute. I agree. We must have an emotional computer. Why don't we know this?

A: Partly because it is an approximating computer, summarizing moment to moment in time but never absolutely summing up and providing an answer. It might tell us that these three sensations, out of the thousands computed, are the ones we should look at. And that would probably change in the next moment—or not. It's not a mathematical enterprise at all, or at least not one involving exact relationships. It's a running serial summary of our experience updated every moment. And it must not only field current sensation but roam through time and make the necessary comparisons with past experience. Millions of bytes of sensation are involved in keeping this constantly summarizing emotional computer functioning.

D: Awesome. We wouldn't begin to know how to build such a computer.

A: We have built ones like the Idiot-Savant's computer where the operation is binary sorting of same/different components. Where I think we would fall apart is in trying to program the thousands of sense particulars from five qualitatively different senses and find an evaluative program that could prioritize them correctly.

D: So the Idiot-Savant uses the emotional computer operation, but his bytes are numbers instead of sensations. Small wonder that going to the store for bread is beyond his ken. We have discovered that the organization of sensation is a far more sophisticated operation than reason will ever be.

A: I think that is truly the case, which is why my emotional computer can walk me across the room, where reason would take a century to coordinate the particulars of that action.

D: I think I now have what I need to continue. Our own mental processing of sensation is far more sophisticated than anything we have dreamed of building rationally. **My cognitive emotion as experienced is the ongoing end product of my emotional computer's simplified summaries and updates. The emotional computer harnesses extraordinarily complex computative power and delivers us a livable world.**

A: No wonder it has no voice as such. It could not slow down enough to employ language and still get the job done.

D: And yet language is where all roads meet, where the emotional meets the rational. **Do you think we can find a structure that joins the emotional and the rational in language?**

A: I think I'm ready. There is now no chance that I will underestimate the complexity or power of the emotional computer just because it humbly and flawlessly serves me in every waking moment. I am sitting on top of some powerful machinery.

D: Agreed. So let's find a home for reason and emotion, some structure that can house both the fluid temporality of emotion and the static spatial order of reason.

A: That structure has to acknowledge the autonomy of both the rational and the emotional systems, doesn't it?

D: Absolutely. There is no way these systems are interchangeable. Yet somehow they form a glorious whole called 'human being'. How in the hell is that possible?

~ CHAPTER III ~

CONSCIOUSNESS AND SELF-CONSCIOUSNESS

Anno: So we have established that the human mental process consists of two autonomous and powerful systems, the sensate emotional computer and the linguistic rational project. These two systems are so different it seems difficult to imagine them working toward the same goals.

Domini: Be that as it may, they are definitely separate and autonomous. It's as if they do not even recognize each other's existence.

A: **And yet they have a meeting ground in language.** Whatever transactions characterize their interactivity will be found to take place in language. What a seemingly imprecise place for this to happen!

D: This is not the meeting of two things, two objects, or two baskets filled with mental activity. It is the cognitive motion that defines them. Be careful. The cognitive interactivity between these two processes must explain why these systems even exist. Their relationship is more important than their autonomy. I suggest we look for a structure that focuses on their relationship.

A: I agree. Two autonomous processes somehow integrate marvelously. What kind of structure allows this to happen? Two minds operating as one.

D: The first step is to try not to speak of them as minds. Try to keep the sense of their dynamics. They are activities.

A: Yes, I do not think this will be a compare-and-contrast dialogue, where reason is red and emotion is blue and together they make purple. Their unity is not manifest in their separate essences.

D: So not 'minds'. Let the rationalists keep this term. What are the alternatives? What is popular these days? Let's turn to everyday speech.

A: **Everyone speaks of being conscious of this or that. Or of doing something 'self-consciously', meaning 'intentionally', I suppose.**

D: But that is a catch-all term. Very non-specific.

A: I wonder about that. Consciousness, the earlier term, sneaked into literacy around five hundred years ago. Later it became the consciousness/self-consciousness dialectic.

D: Was it just a convenience? It slips into usage and now it is on everyone's lips? Freud probably made it popular.

A: Freud with all his rational little boxes like 'id', 'ego', 'superego', and the 'unconscious'? Perhaps, but the terms 'consciousness' and 'self-consciousness' predate his usage and now seem to mean something different.

D: Yes. The terms themselves are very handy. They have subtly taken over as a picture of our mental dynamic.

A: True, and with little or no opposition from the scholars. Maybe these terms are more sophisticated than anyone thinks.

D: All right. Let's make an assumption. Let's assume that consciousness/self-consciousness is the terminology we have been searching for. What does that immediately tell you?

A: Despite its popularity and accessibility, I would have to say that latent in this dialectic is the most sophisticated of all philosophical structures. It is sort of like the invention of the wheel. Everyone uses the wheel, and doesn't question why, but there is no more sophisticated tool in use. If consciousness/self-consciousness can put reason and emotion together, there must be a great deal about it that is not known.

D: My thought also. **The consciousness/self-consciousness dialectic is known to all, but its dynamic must be very complex.**

A: If this dialectic can bring order to the interface between reason and emotion, it must be the most formidable philosophical structure since ontology. Like Being and Non-Being, the fact that it lends itself to hundreds of interpretations serves only to underscore its importance. **Knowing what we now do about the emotional computer, we will need to create a very specific structure here, because the emotional computer gives altogether new meaning to the relationship between consciousness and self-consciousness. If that relationship is to change, the whole familiar structure of mental processing must change.**

49

D: Perhaps the most important understanding of this dialectic was waiting for us. We have spent great energy making reason and emotion equal in all respects. This may be the missing key to understanding what this relationship is.

A: I'm for it. Let's try it . What do we know superficially about these terms 'consciousness' and 'self-consciousness' ?

D: They convey motion and the experiential better than 'mind'. They have a temporal sense of awareness attached to them. They lean toward the subjective and away from mental processing seen as an object. They are also dual where 'mind' is singular.

A: That helps, but I want to be even more basic. The first thing I notice is that self-consciousness is aware of consciousness but not vice versa.

D: So we start with a very fundamental asymmetry. I predict this asymmetry will be the key to the relationship. The overall structure is an intimate cooperation between inherently dissimilar components, not oppositional but complementary. This is like asking an elephant and a rabbit to perform tasks together. Each can summon its own intricate capabilities for the common task, but neither has anything but a minimal understanding of the capabilities of the other. It is what they together achieve, and not what they separately represent, that matters. And what they together achieve may be beyond anything either of them ever thought possible. The focus is only secondarily on who the rabbit and the elephant are; the primary focus and interest is how they together achieve anything. Such a structure is necessarily dynamic.

A: Again, we must look at the way they move, not what they are.

D: Let's begin with consciousness. When we were discussing the animistic period of human development, we noted that this was the purest example of emotion dominant in mental processing. There was little language and little reason as yet. Consciousness seems to resemble that. Consciousness seems to be simply the awareness of felt quality. It has no voice of its own.

A: And the animistic period precedes the development of self-consciousness. Let's say tentatively that consciousness is the emotional computer.

D: Let me try it. That would mean that consciousness is always in motion, a sea of feeling and sensation, an experiential and environmental awareness whose goal is the existential integration of an individual's life. It would be wholly dynamic and pre-verbal. The egoistic 'I' would not exist for it. Consciousness is the emotional computer!

A: Let's see if other disciplines would agree. I need to surround the equation between consciousness and the emotional computer with a sense of how the mind evolved. Animism was a stage in that development. I'd like to see how sociobiology and particularly brain neurology would confirm or deny this conclusion. Carl Sagan's *The Dragons of Eden* would be useful here.

D: OK. We can start with the hemispheres of the brain. The oldest hemisphere is the right one. It has its roots in the limbic system and is regarded as the seat of emotion. As the cerebral cortices and the temporal lobes later developed, the right hemisphere remained the seat of emotional thinking. It is apperceptive and holistic. Its apparent goal is to form unities of emotional experience.

A: And it never stops. It is intermittently dominant in daylight hours depending on the individual and what he is doing. It is wholly dominant in dreams. The dream state today perhaps most closely corresponds to the animistic period of man's development.

D: The left cerebral cortex was a cellular redundancy in evolution, a mirror for the animistic right cerebral cortex, but one with no assigned function. This is common in biological evolution. It subsequently became the center of language development. As such it became even later the home of reason.

A: The hemispheres are connected by the corpus callosum whose function appears to be communication between the hemispheres. This interaction is little understood. In fact, that interaction is what we are trying to think through, is it not?

D: Very much so. The hemispheric brain interaction difficulties are compounded by the fact that bilateral symmetry is skewed. The right ear, eye, and hand report to the left brain and vice-versa. The reason for this is not known, but it again suggests a more complex relationship between the hemispheres than simple one-to-one correspondence.

A: Additionally, the left hemisphere language center is not oriented holistically but tends to break things down into parts. So we are in line with brain neurology. Consciousness is located in the right brain and is the seat of sensation and emotion. I think we can allow the equation between the emotional computer and consciousness to stand, and allow that they originate neurologically in the right brain.

D: That left brain temporal lobe develops later and is the seat of language development. Language development seems to correspond with the development of self-consciousness.

A: And since consciousness continues to compute in much the same way as it always has, it was up to self-consciousness, as it became more useful and complex, to evolve a relationship to consciousness.

D: It evolved an 'I' as the standing center of itself, an 'I' over and against the world around it. This subject/object structure can then compartmentalize the world around it into spatial empirical components. As it improves its ability to compartmentalize the world, the world of science comes into being.

A: All well and good, but that doesn't help us focus on the relationship between consciousness and self-consciousness. Biologists are still staring at the corpus callosum link between hemispheres and wondering how it works.

D: At least it confirms two separate systems at all levels, which somehow work in concert. We needed to know that. Now we need to get simple-minded for a bit. What can we say about this relationship?

A: Well, self-consciousness gives orders to consciousness.

D: Like what?

A: It's the place of the 'I' command center. 'I will now walk across the room'.

D: And consciousness then carries out these orders?

A: Yes. Consciousness has neither will nor desire.

D: Does self-consciousness tell consciousness how to walk across the room? Or is consciousness for the most part in charge of enacting the command?

A: I see. Self-consciousness could not begin to direct this action in detail. It simply gives the command and consciousness has to interpret and enact the command in light of all environmental factors present at the time.

D: OK. So we are really not speaking of a Master/Slave relationship. Self-consciousness tries to understand the path it wishes to follow and directs consciousness accordingly. Tentatively, we can say self-consciousness has will and chooses to direct. Consciousness does what it has to, but although it enacts self-consciousness, it must interpret the action entirely by its own dictates.

A: Come at it from another angle. They meet in language. How does that occur?

D: 'Language' is a loaded term. Language includes the whole spectrum from fast moving connotative words where emotion predominates, such as 'scared out of my wits' to almost static rational denotations such as 'the sum of the square of the hypotenuse'. Let's track an emotional understanding linearly as it moves through consciousness and into self-consciousness.

A: OK. Consciousness computes the sensory data of our felt experience. Its focus is movement and patterns of movement. When it discovers a possibly significant pattern in its sensate computation, it will go on to explore just how significant the pattern might be. Its goal is to determine what is important at any and all levels. Its goal is intuitive understanding. These journeys have different magnitudes and complexity, depending on the degree to which the significance can expand. Some of these significances resolve quickly; they are noteworthy but negligible, meaning they will not be brought before self-consciousness. Some of these journeys result in the kinds of significance that become maximally present in our awareness. This intense presencing is somehow thrust before self-consciousness.

D: Good. The first awareness that self-consciousness has of such significance is a sudden but general notice taken of something important. Self-consciousness immediately tries to verbalize this pre-verbal importance presented to it by consciousness. This is where consciousness and self-consciousness meet. Self-consciousness uses the highly emotive end of language to articulate what is important and is then in charge of analyzing and dissecting just what is so important.

A: And as we noted in discussing the emotional system of consciousness, these significances may be thrust into self-consciousness as emergencies ('I smell smoke') or be strongly invitational ('You will be very interested in this…').

D: At this point self-consciousness has options. It can become a passive watcher and follow the developing significance, adding language when the opportunity presents itself. Or it can take charge of the significance and begin to concretize it using objective language. The difference in the two stances devolves around the question of whether the presencing has summarized itself emotionally or is still developing. Self-consciousness decides whether it is dealing with finished emotional product or a process still in development. The decision is based on the motion involved. Language begins to retard and stop the motion of the significance, so it must be applied judiciously.

A: Agreed. Felt motion that comes to one's attention must be assessed as to its degree of significance. How urgent or powerfully invitational is the message from consciousness? After making this assessment, self-consciousness can then articulate *what* is important by giving it linguistic and spatial dimension.

D: It then has to move the significance through a language range from the connotative to the denotative. The applicability of the significance may summarize at any point along that pathway. Some significances may stop at 'Your fly is open' while others may go on and on, resulting in a new painting, a new geometry, or a new way to teach autistic children. Reason is not always needed. This need for reason is controlled by the empirical relevance of the original significance.

A: I think so. Reason here is almost a spatial zoom lens. It breaks the importance down into smaller and smaller pieces, continually re-assembling the whole to see what it has got. Its overall goal is to determine the applicability of the significance.

D: And we cannot forget that self-consciousness exercises veto power within this process. If I am driving down an icy road with white-knuckle concentration when it suddenly occurs to me that there is a new element in my relationship with my wife, I will undoubtedly decide that this conscious intrusion can wait. I have to watch my driving. I can put this on hold, but it may not presence with the same power later. Still, it is better to put this on hold than run off the road.

A: We've all been there. I am beginning to understand why I have this insistent fascination with knives but have to put this on hold because the report my boss is waiting for must be finished in the next fifteen minutes. No choice.

D: What's important about the veto, though, is that it is not simply used as an expedient measure. Our contemporary society has a pro-rational prejudice that questions the value of many of these significant intrusions by consciousness, since they are simply emotional interruptions. **Our society seems to feel that blocking these emotional interruptions leaves one freer to reason.**

A: You cannot blame our society. Everyone is offered sixteen years of educational training in how to be analytic and rational. How many students are ever trained to recognize and evaluate significance? People in our society will turn down a lot of invitations which might change their world because the invitations are 'only emotional'.

D: Or because the occurrence of something suddenly significant is threatening. It could lead one out of control, since the outcome of such an emotional journey is unpredictable.

A: Full circle. 'Creativity' is certainly being rationally 'out of control'. The more reason becomes the adversary of emotion, the more likely we are to ignore all but the most urgent significances presented by consciousness, the result being that we refuse our creative impulses.

D: So self-consciousness chooses what tasks language will take on. In addition to whatever it is currently assessing, it must listen to the intrusions of consciousness and decide if or whether to develop them linguistically. Self-consciousness is definitely our land animal. It can stand in one place, stop the motion, and evaluate the picture. If it is too rational, it can refuse to listen to anything presented by consciousness except an emergency.

A: Ideally, though, without the extreme rational prejudice of our contemporary world, there would always be a high reciprocity between consciousness and self-consciousness. Self-consciousness would spend a great deal of time listening for new significance, and balance listening with linguistic action. The two facets of the mental process have in reality one goal: to constantly integrate change into a useful adaptation to the world as lived and experienced.

D: Which means if the relationship is rigid, the whole person suffers. There must be a fluid relationship between equals, one open to constant adaptation. Consciousness does not carelessly present significance. It has no will in the matter. And self-consciousness must choose both to listen and to act. To do so it must also be conversant with the whole range of language from the emotional to the rational.

A: The relationship between reason and emotion within the consciousness/self-consciousness dialectic is, in the last analysis, a personal one. It is an emotional relationship. As such, this is the place where the epistemological and the ethical meet. The interaction has a sacred quality. This mental relationship between two autonomous processes is quintessentially human and ethical.

D: And yet there is an impersonal quality to consciousness considered as the emotional computer. The ethical dimension that determines the quality of the interrelation must be determined within self-consciousness. But how? How do human freedom and the ability to choose the type of relationship come about?

A: Consciousness has memory, but its memory is intrinsic to its processing; its memory is part of its computer. Self-consciousness also has memory, but a memory greatly rigidified as the time line of the past. And for this reason it can stand outside time and be spatial, but there is a cost. It must remain continually aware of, as Sartre puts it, the "nihilating upsurge of the present". Its sense of the past is reified, so that the present continually destroys who the person is and thrusts the person into the unknown and undetermined present. The present, then, for self-consciousness, must be seen as continuous choice. Human freedom is located here. Choice belongs to the land animal, self-consciousness, because of its capacity to objectify time past.

D: Including all personal choices, such as the choice to be creative or rational.

A: It can choose to listen when consciousness intrudes and says 'This is important'. It can also choose to remain the observer, attempting to understand the patterns and rules governing its existence and learning to apply them. Isolation from consciousness is necessary in some instances. Fortunately, consciousness continues to operate the organism while all this self-conscious evaluation takes place.

D: You state that last observation blithely, but it poses a question. How do we know consciousness and self-consciousness are coeval? Maybe they alternate or displace one another.

A: Conscious activity never stops, even in sleep. It couldn't. It must control and integrate sensate experience from moment to moment. The organism never stops feeling. Self-consciousness is intermittent. To startle oneself into self-conscious awareness that one has been performing an involved task is to return to self-consciousness. During the task one was simply conscious. Alternatively, I might have been washing dishes and simultaneously focused on planning my weekend, in which case both self-consciousness and consciousness are operating simultaneously without reference to each other. I become aware of this simultaneity when I break my reverie and realize the dishes are done. Who did the dishes? Consciousness. Who was in a reverie? Self-consciousness. Self-consciousness can access its freedom because consciousness is minding the store.

D: Does consciousness have an 'I'?

A: No—and yes. **Consciousness is the emotionally integrated person who does not know himself. It has no center as such. The 'I' belongs to self-consciousness, which stands still in time and space and is aware of its static continuity as observed**.

D: Self-consciousness is the true integrator of the human being.

A: No, only at one level. Without the dialectic between the two there is no self and no self-consciousness.

D: Then the type of ethical relationship between them is determined by self-consciousness in terms of the way it chooses to relate. Ideally self-consciousness is listening to consciousness as much as it is displacing it, doing both to create the language picture of its world.

A: I believe this relationship is freely chosen by self-consciousness. Yet if we see this relationship in all its complexity, as we have been doing, it is apparent that these two modes are married in every sense. If self-consciousness does not remain intimately related to conscious intrusions into its world, the whole organism suffers.

D: **Yes, and I think it is time to dispense with the term 'dialectic' used to describe the relationship. Consciousness heads for the beauty of intuitive completion in intense presencing. Self-consciousness tries for integrated order including the inputs of consciousness. It is no use trying to determine who rules here. The ethics of these mental processes are found in their overwhelming need to dialogue.**

A: **A dialogue rather than a dialectic, because their relationship is profoundly emotional. The first ethical principle of self-consciousness is** to discover beauty in the dialogue with consciousness. The goal of the dialogue is beauty. Self-relationship is governed by the ethics of the beautiful. Regardless of the asymmetry of the relationship, where self-consciousness appears to be directing and consciousness appears to be selfless, this relationship is the model for all others in life. This relationship is where we become more human or less human.

D: And it is set up that way in the very structure of the dialogue.

A: We were listening, weren't we?

D: We have created a house for reason and emotion: consciousness and self-consciousness.

A: Not a house. A dynamically complex love relationship to which reason and emotion belong.

D: Where one has no meaning apart from the other.

A: They relate to perform a single action: human being.

D: Are we re-creating the human mental process?

A: I think we have. Our dialogue continues to expand the dialogue within ourselves. I see that as the dialogue continues to expand it must take in a subject so central that all other roads lead to it.

D: Creativity. We are creating creativity. We must understand intuition!

A: Can that be done in dialogue?

D: How else, I ask you. Haven't you been listening? The Socratic Boogie goes on and on…

~ CHAPTER IV ~

Intuition

Anno: I believe we are out on a long limb. We have made intuition the climax of the emotional computations of consciousness. We also used it to describe the interactivity in which consciousness and self-consciousness meet.

Domini: Intuition is carrying a heavy burden. Unless we can provide a clear delineation of what takes place in intuition, our whole description of the mental process is in jeopardy.

A: One thing is clear. We have decided that intuition is a-rational and that it belongs to consciousness. I still believe this is true. Let us look at the historical roots of this discussion in philosophy and see if we are at odds with the arguments. We seem to be culminating and integrating ideas more than we refute them.

D: Intuition is one of the largest problems in the history of philosophy, especially since I believe we are linking it to the largest of all problems: transcendence.

A: Intuition has always had to do with the acquisition of new understanding or knowledge. Transcendence is much the same. How does the human mind transcend its own understanding? More simply put, how does the mind unify its disparate understandings? How do we acquire new knowledge?

D: The answer to this question gives a philosophy tremendous leverage.

A: You mean leverage in the Archimedean sense? Give me a sufficient lever and I will move the world? Certainly. Great philosophies have considerably advanced our knowledge of the human condition, but they have been unable to tell us how the human mind learns. Not because they haven't tried, either.

D: I think the respect for rational thought governed too tyrannically. The assumption was always that reason was the highest faculty of mind and somehow it should have been able to solve the problem of transcendence.

A: I think we should highlight and summarize these efforts. It is clear to me that the first great products of Greek thought were the syllogism and the dialectic. They both attempt to produce a unity of thought out of disparate parts and both fail. It took a long time to see this.

D: The syllogism consisted of three parts: 'All men are mortal/Socrates is a man/ Socrates is mortal'. This was the early rationalist attempt to make two thoughts produce a third, in which that third part was a new understanding. Its failure seems to be its linguistic rigidity.

A: The syllogism makes an assumption about language, that if the words are precise enough, the meaning will be precise. It deeply needs to believe that there are words with one and only one meaning.

D: The thinking is that if words like 'mortal' and 'man' have one and only one meaning, these linguistic bricks can be used to build a house of logical knowledge.

A: And words, as history has shown, are not bricks. Numbers yes, words no. Words cannot be made completely static and spatial. Words always have a context of meaning. As we noted earlier, all words have an emotional or experiential component, regardless of how abstract they might be. A word such as 'rigidity' has its own emotional context and connotes. It moves, however slowly.

D: So the bricks move too much and the house tumbles down. Logic can only succeed if words can be wholly quantitative, and none are. It was up to the dialecticians to point this out.

A: They regarded the great pairs in philosophy as qualitative rather than quantitative, pairs such as time/space, subject/object, and one/ many. They showed that the pillars of philosophy were themselves in motion, were to some extent always connotative and therefore 'in motion'. They took words like 'being' and explored their myriad associations, demonstrating that such terms can never be wholly quantified. These two approaches have been arguing with each other for millennia without success.

D: Why were these approaches so persistent? Where does the drive to substantiate them come from?

A: There is a fundamental reason for this perseverance. Logic tries quantitatively to combine two things into a third. Dialectics tries to resolve two things into one. Three is the magic number here.

D: I've wondered. Why isn't the syllogism four-part or six-part? All the comparisons are two combined into a third. Why is 'three' the magic number?

A: There is a non-verbalized understanding here that controls the discussion. The belief here is that if two things can be combined into a third thing, the principle of new knowledge or transcendence will have been demonstrated.

D: So what is this belief based on? Why is it so rigid?

A: This conviction is based on a feature of language, particularly rational language. Simply put, the mind cannot compare three things simultaneously, which truism is beyond argument. Let me show you. Take the three primary colors and compare them.

D: Well, I can say that red is warmer than blue. Yellow is warmer than blue and not as warm as red. Where does this go?

A: Was that really a three-way comparison?

D: I thought so.

A: Did you compare three colors simultaneously?

D: I see. No, I actually paired them across a quality. Red is warmer than yellow, red is warmer than blue. How warm are blue and yellow relative to each other? I cannot compare them except as pairs, can I?

A: No. And this demonstrates a limit of the linguistic self-consciousness. A simultaneous three-way comparison is beyond its capabilities. Three is a limiting condition, which is why philosophical analysis has always reasoned on those terms. The implicit awareness has always been that two is workable and three is the limit. What has always driven the transcendence issue is the conviction that if two things could be somehow combined into a third thing, new knowledge would result. This is in turn based on the conviction that new knowledge does occur, so there must be a way to reason it.

D: The explanation would have to be verbal and rational, since this is where higher thought occurs. The rational prejudice again.

A: Yes, whereas we are assuming that this new knowledge occurs preverbally and sensorily in consciousness, an a-rational system.

D: So if we are right, philosophy continued to look in the wrong place for the right thing.

A: It's not that simple. Every great philosophy mentions and discusses intuitional understanding. It was always regarded as important in some unspecified way. For our purposes, the longest running definition of intuition is used in Plato and on throughout the Middle Ages up through Descartes. Intuition was defined as a "clear and certain percept". This definition is definitely visual and it in turn dates back to Plato's understanding that intuition illuminated the mind with new understanding.

D: Yes, and that understanding has always posed two problems. The truth of an intuition was regarded as self-convicting and self-evident, needing no further validation. And it obviously originated in the sensory realm. The first problem was how could an understanding be true or knowledge if it had not been reasoned? As the rational prejudice grew, the existence of intuition became more problematic. Secondly, how could anything emerging from the sensory realm yield real knowledge? The denigration of the sensory as an inferior arena of knowledge was well established by Descartes.

A: So a kind of truth exists that needs no verification, but its origins are sensory and inferior for that reason. Reason, on the other hand, cannot produce a logic that has the convicting power of intuition, although it is assumed to be the superior form of knowledge. Tools, technology, and science, after all, are rational.

D: And this adversarial struggle between reason and intuition continues to the present day.

A: For specific reasons. Intuitions appear to be linguistic because their intensity causes rapid articulation immediately after they occur. If one regards both intuition and reason as linguistic, and reason is the superior tool, philosophy could not understand why it couldn't produce a rational form of intuition.

D: So the assumptions regarding intuition are false. The assumptions make reason and intuition two halves of a whole. Combine them somehow and you have met the criterion: a new self-convicting rational understanding.

A: Exactly. And we are about to proffer the idea that new understanding does not occur within language at all, but in the pre-verbal sensory computations of consciousness. We have definitely stepped up to bat. Where do we go from here?

D: Hegel is one philosopher who understood most of this problem and took it almost as far as it can be taken rationally. He is helpful in setting the stage for us.

A: Yes. When we leave traditional philosophy, he should have the last word. Here is the one philosopher who combined superb rational capabilities with an undying love for what we have called "cognitive motion".

D: We are talking about the epistemology of the *Phenomenology*, correct?

A: Yes. You and I understand this differently than most philosophers, but that is not our problem. Hegel's epistemology is temporal. It is in motion. It is series-form. It is about intuition.

D: Hegel's various terms for it are "past-present-future", "thesis-antithesis-synthesis", "bud-blossom-fruit", and "being-becoming-become". Superficially it looks like an attempt at a syllogism.

A: Yes, but each phase of the three represents a motion, not a part, a quality and not a quantity. The third motion temporally represents the unification of the other two. We need to focus on the quality of the movement. Let me show you something: 1,2,3,5,6,7,9…

D: A series, where numbers follow thrice in succession and then add two.

A: Notice that your summary has nothing to do with the quantities and everything to do with the quality of their movement. Hegel has left quantity altogether. The three-part motion of the trithesis controls how his noun subjects are integrated. In addition, there is also a temporal atomism at work here. Each of the three basic epistemic motions is itself composed of three motions. The epistemic base unit is a nine-phased motion. These nine motions describe the compossible combinations of our time sense.

D: Every present is itself, was a future, and becomes a past. Every past is itself, and was a future and a present. Every future will become a present and eventually a past. So the structure of consciousness in Hegel is one nine-phased temporal moment. The interactive logic of this moment controls all material under discussion.

A: Exactly! By the time the reader has traveled through numerous tritheses and reaches the peak of "Absolute Self-Consciousness" he is supposed to have understood that this is an epistemically repeating series: 1,2,3,1,4,5,1,6,7…. Each beginning term of each trithesis is the same as all the other beginning terms. Each fourth member is in reality a first member. Thus the whole of the *Phenomenology*, as well as each trithetic discussion, is a single temporal moment. The qualitative movement of this triple interaction controls the entire hierarchy of the thought, from the smallest to the largest groupings.

D: The dynamics of this three-fold movement are then critical. How is the interaction established?

A: A thesis is offered as the first term. The second is compared and contrasted to the first, but more important is its motion. It performs a double temporal negation. It is not the first term by virtue of succeeding that first term in time, and it is not the third term because it precedes it. The first term is its past and the third term is its future. The second term is critical.

D: It seems the third term is critical. It unites the other two. Hegel was attempting a rational description of intuition. He knows that his 'synthesis', the third term, represents the principle by which the first two are united. This would be a classical syllogistic stance except that these three components are temporal motions and not parts. What makes me certain that he is trying to create a logic of intuition is that at the point where the second term is about to move on to the third, Hegel indicates that this second term must now be "sublated and preserved".

A: Archaic language signifying what?

D: The second term is put on hold until its motion is complete in the third motion. It is not dispensed with, but literally 'put down under and held in the mind'.

A: So that it can do what?

D: This is what Hegel never solved. At the point where the second term becomes the third, the intuition is complete. Hegel knew that the most rationally enigmatic facet of intuition is that the duration of an intuition cannot be predicted. And his is a temporal epistemology. As such, the third term could take five minutes or five years to complete itself. He knew reason could not control this duration. Intuition, regardless of its logic, takes its own good time. Hegel's recognition of this is in the phrase "sublated and preserved", meaning 'the second term is held in the mind until the uniting action of the third term takes place'. He could not construct a binding linkage between the first two terms and the third, except to say that eventually the third motion unites the other two.

A: So his description is true to intuition basically, but the rational approach cannot work. He would have needed an emotional analysis.

D: Which Hegel would not permit within his thinking. What he also realized about intuition is that it deals intimately with repeating pattern. It was his conviction that if he repeated the three fold pattern of the logic enough times, the reader would intuit that Hegel was writing a logic of intuition.

A: So although he understood that intuition involves patterns of movement, he made the mistake of thinking that these patterns were linguistic and rational rather than emotional. Is this what scholars have referred to as "The Secret of Hegel"?

D: I believe so. Understanding the *Phenomenology* requires that the reader has to intuit—and there was no guarantee that he would—that

Hegel was creating an epistemology of intuition. In other words, the success of the Phenomenology was dependent on the reader intuiting that the subject of the work was intuition.

A: And depending on the individual, this might work or it might not.

D: Mostly it didn't work. Scholars did not see the implications of what Hegel was attempting, although our explanation is the only way to make sense of his epistemology.

A: But you are also saying he was wrong.

D: I am saying that Hegel described the process of intuition across numerous examples, and that is the extent to which reason can address an a-rational structure. He sees it from the outside. Intuition may not occur within language or reason, but it can definitely be felt and experienced. **Hegel was trying to rationalize the experience by showing that it was accessible through sufficient repetition; he should have tried to create it. Still, he gives us a leg up. He knows the process is temporally dynamic. He knows its duration cannot be controlled. He knows that repetition of pattern often triggers intuition.** He knows that, however transcendence leading to new knowledge is achieved, it must involve the interlocking motions of qualities experienced and cannot be a combination of quantitative parts.

A: But he will not let these motions be emotional; he retains the rational and the linguistic bias.

D: Yes. He wants to rationally control transcendence instead of creating it, and fails to do so—because it cannot be done. I believe the most important contribution Hegel made to the understanding of intuition is what I have called 'series-form' thought, which explores the structure of qualitative motion. I think we will be returning to this construct when we try to understand the emotional computer.

A: So Hegel takes us as far as we can go rationally. Can we ballpark intuition now? It doesn't mean what Hegel meant, yet it has had all kinds of uses historically. I want to address the multifaceted usage of the term.

D: Agreed. Let's see. **Intuition always means some kind of significant insight.**

A: Which means it always refers to new understanding. **Real transcendent knowledge occurs here and not in the rational domain.**

D: Let the philosophical terms go. We are after the same thing philosophy was after, but we cannot use that terminology. Let's move to the language of experience.

A: OK. How do I experience intuition? Most notably as an 'Aha' or 'Eureka', a burst of understanding. But aren't there other kinds of intuition?

D: Feminine intuition has a long history, I suspect because the emotional arena has traditionally been the property of women. Intuition involves all kinds of patterns of felt movement. Hegel was right on that score. Here's one. I'm standing on a street corner watching someone walking away from me down the street when I suddenly recognize who the person is. This is not rational. I am intuiting a sensory pattern of movement, recognizing the whole.

A: Then there are the intuitions artists have in creating a work of art, ones that are somehow accessible to the hearer or viewer. The artist is someone who finds a way to showcase his intuition using his media.

D: What ties all these intuitive reckonings together? Are they all intuition? Can we deal with a concrete example here?

A: Yes. I'll borrow Kant's numbers for the example: 7+5=12. I think it can show us that intuition definitely occurs, but not what it is *per se*. We can then go on from there.

D: Hegel would like this. A child is told that somehow the seven and the five become twelve. He is given numerous other examples showing the same thing. He knows that five is different from seven and different from twelve, but doesn't understand how one winds up with twelve. He does not understand the 'plus' sign.

A: Exactly. He works the process from example to example, mostly memorizing the answers. He works with apples and oranges. One day his 'Aha' occurs. He understands what he is doing. This is a great moment for a teacher to observe, especially if the student has taken quite a while to 'Aha'. Many times the child will then begin to do over again all the sums he has memorized, but this time with the understanding of what he is doing.

D: And the teacher knows that the child has intuited what addition is because she intuits what the child has done.

A: That's clear enough. Intuition is the only way the child could understand this process. It is clearly a new understanding for him. The question remains: What is he doing?

D: I think we can definitely say the recognition of moving pattern is important here.

A: Yes. Somehow by repeating the examples the pattern manifests itself for him. Hegel was right on that score. But why? And this mathematical example may be misleading. We must understand intuition as a process that combines associations from any and all media, not just mathematics.

D: Agreed. Do you think we can look at the emotional computer again? There is something in this series-form process of Hegel's that relates to the emotional system.

A: So for a bit you want to try to extend Hegelian thought and see how far analysis can take us. All right. But you realize that at some point we need to examine intuition as experienced rather than as reasoned.

D: I need to go as far as I can to see *why* the spark jumps, why the intuition is new and a surprise. I have been doodling while we have been in dialogue. Take a look at this: 1,2,3,4,5,6,7,8,9,10,11,…

A: You seem to be showing me a series but it looks like you are just counting.

D: Let's say these numbers represent felt sensations occurring in experience. The movement of these sensations presents no surprise or interest. They are known. So far it is simply the recognition of a known pattern. Remember, we are focusing on the qualitative motion between the numbers or 'sensations'. What would you predict to be the next sensation or number?

A: Obviously, I would expect it to be twelve.

D: Let's say it is actually this: 1,2,3,4,5,6,7,8,9,10,11,16…

A: Then I have to reassess the motion of the whole sequence from the beginning. Let me see. The description is more complex. Three consecutive integers followed by a fourth, the fourth doubling each time. Now I am interested in these sensations.

D: My thought exactly. Rather than the expected pattern, an anomalous sensation or integer appears. I take this event to be, for consciousness, the beginning of the intuitional process. Something significant has happened. We could even call this a small intuition in and of itself, for we have not simply changed one number, but qualitatively changed the whole movement configuration of the series. The mind is forced to reshuffle its understanding.

A: You mean the emotional computer, which with the sensation '16' is forced to interphasically race back and forth through time to determine if it has ever encountered this pattern. This '16' has caused the realignment of familiar patterning into a new unity, which is an intuition. For the moment, let's say that consciousness takes this pattern and researches it. Consciousness is 'interested' and computes and awaits the next sensation in the series.

D: Not only that, as the feeling of discovered significance starts to grow, an anticipatory interest also starts to grow. This could be a minor anomaly and a minor intuition, or its significance could keep growing. The contingencies are how much comparative research consciousness must do and the future of the pattern as it evolves in experience.

A: So an intuitional process is launched by the '16' in the series.

D: Yes. And let's make the next integer '17' to further complexicate the series.

A: OK, so the next three integers after the doubling must sequentially follow the doubling: 1,2,3,4,5,6,7,8,9,10,11,16,17,18,19,32… Another anomaly has occurred.

D: And this can keep happening indefinitely. I think we have seen enough to know where we want to go. The seventeen represents the second point where consciousness must reassess the entire quality of movement it is observing. The series is becoming more complex and interesting. It is becoming more significant because it involves more and more sensations.

A: Unless this is already a known pattern of movement, such as recognizing a person you know.

D: True, but let's say the pattern is new. Consciousness must visit all clusters of emotional experience in which each anomaly occurs and visit any experience in which they both occur.

A: That could take a long time. It's a good thing that consciousness is a computer.

D: That's not the half of it. If the next term in the series is not '32', another series has presented itself.

A: What bothers me is you are using linear movement as a model. Consciousness might be and probably is assessing multiple patterned movements concurrently.

D: You are right. It definitely shows me that we are looking at a dimensionality of computative complexity which we could not rationally follow.

A: We could probably follow it mathematically if we were only dealing with numbers. At least our current computers could.

D: Yes, but if these numbers are actually different sensations coming in from five qualitatively different senses, how would you even begin to prioritize and pattern this input?

A: It boggles my mind. The emotional computer is awesome. So when do I self-consciously know when consciousness has completed the intuition?

D: Go back to my simplistic series example. I think that by the point of the second series anomaly an emotional bell is ringing. More computative emotional energy must now be poured into solving the pattern. The bell is just an image. It stands for an intensification of effort as experienced, and the growing presence of this particular emotional sequence.

A: Accepted. And this bell-ringing grows until it intrudes into self-consciousness. Self-consciousness is becoming aware of something of interest. A new pattern of association is possibly in the making.

D: And still self-consciousness may ignore the bell. It may be occupied elsewhere in language, thought, or action. Consciousness itself may have forced self-consciousness to ignore the bell. Perhaps it threw an emergency pattern in front of self-consciousness just before the new pattern began to appear. Or the significance of the new pattern may not have grown enough for the bell to be loud or insistent, in which case self-consciousness continues to stay involved elsewhere.

A: But let's assume self-consciousness begins to listen, accepting the invitation to watch consciousness find the real pattern. I have to think that self-consciousness begins to watch because something interesting has occurred and language is beginning to be created to identify it.

D: Agreed. It could be 'The car is making an unusual sound' or 'What message does that poem have for me?' One locates the interest and allows it to grow.

A: So the tough question returns. When has it grown enough? When does it burst into the 'Aha' or 'Eureka'. What event could possibly cause this?

D: I do not think the intensity of the intuitional climax is simply a matter of its suddenness. Other factors are involved. The weight and density of the emotions in the series being computed may entail a complex journey for consciousness. Translated, this results in an intuition with greater scope of meaning. And one does not need to be in constant self-conscious attendance to the significance. More than likely the journey itself is intermittent. One keeps looking in on the process because the significance continues to intensify.

A: Self-consciousness suspects an intuition is immanent because a great deal of emotional energy continues to intrude on it. The bell is getting louder.

D: Yes. Some half –seen significance can dog self-consciousness for days or months without ever coming to center stage. The emotional computer slogs on. The series simply appears to be complex and still moving.

A: But there comes a point where a climax occurs.

D: Yes, and perhaps without self-conscious preamble. Many people have awakened in the morning with a powerful intuition sitting there in their minds. Consciousness summarized the series during the night.

A: But the series we used was simplistic. How does consciousness know when to summarize a complex series? How does self-consciousness know that this has occurred?

D: I understand what you are getting at, but the series or multiple series never stop evolving. The question is why self-consciousness *thinks* that the series has summarized in some final fashion.

A: All emotional series go on being recomputed for a lifetime. Only death stops the series from evolving. Self-consciousness must be governed by emotion in this situation, a degree of either presence or significance.

D: I believe you have it. The 'Aha' is an overflow of emotion, emotion powerfully seeking language. If a change in the series involves sufficient emotional reconstruction, it presences itself in self-consciousness to such an extreme degree as to occupy its whole attention. The series analogy is helpful but not past this point. **What causes a powerful emotional reaction in self-consciousness?**

A: **Speechlessness. This is the real power of consciousnesss. To presence feeling to the extent that self-consciousness loses the power of speech explains the 'Aha'.**

D: **Self-consciousness is stunned by the rearrangement of emotion. It is initially speechless.**

A: Because although it is probably familiar with all these emotions, their new structure in the intuition has no name. It is in reality a new experience and self-consciousness is not related to it.

D: And our series analogy is still relevant. Faced with the stunning quality of this new configuration of familiar cognates, self-consciousness must parallel the journey consciousness has just taken and re-relate itself to this new intuition.

A: The series form gives me the best emotional sense of that impact intuition has. Familiar numbers—sensations—are reconfigured in a pattern that I do not recognize. These familiar sensations have come together as an impactive unity, meaning I know the pattern is coherent, just as I knew the number series had become a new series. What adds to this reaction in self-consciousness is the pressure of speech. **To mentally see a pattern that has no language corollary convinces me that it is new and truly significant. The pressure created by the desire to articulate this new pattern only adds to the emotional force of the intuition.**

D: And for self-consciousness the first order of business after the emotional impact of the intuition is to articulate it. In effect, self-consciousness must build language bridges between the intuition and all known previous experience. This outworking can take a great deal of time. I have heard it called 'unpacking the suitcase' of the intuition.

A: Yes. After all, as new experience, the intuition is not related to the experience of the individual, not in the form in which it appears.

D: And, as self-consciousness articulates the intuition, it begins to relate the intuition to the world. It discovers its utility and relevance. It analyzes and reasons it. It begins with reactive connotative language that tries to get a handle on what has happened and moves gradually to more denotative analytic speech as it breaks down the components of the intuition. At some point it reasons it, and relates it to the empirical world, finally understanding the utility of the intuition.

A: I'm guessing that intuitions are somewhat thematic. This has always bothered me. Now I can see that the level of sophistication of the intuition probably follows the interests of the individual. A philosopher has philosopher's intuitions. A musician has musician's intuitions.

D: As well as the general ones everyone has.

A: But my point is that mathematicians are still debating whether they reason or intuit. Again, given the sophistication of intuition and its thematic quality, I realize that intuitions occur at every level of abstraction.

D: Mobius was a fine example of this.

A: Yes, the Mobius Strip.

D: Mobius notices that his belt has one twist in it. He takes it off and twists it once and clasps it and observes. He is intrigued by the flat plane of the belt as it becomes first its own underside and then its topside. A bell is sounding. He takes the invitation. This is a mathematician's invitation. He is a mathematician.

A: He must have been. I would have just told him to stop playing with his belt and get on with his life.

D: But eventually he intuits the core of his interest. There is no geometry that can describe the plane of the belt. Is it two dimensional or three? Finally he has the climactic intuition which eventually results in new non-Euclidean geometries.

A: So the belt was interesting and significant, but until the intuition burst on his self-consciousness, forcing him to articulate what happened, the relevance of his interest would not be apparent to him.

D: Each of us intuits along lines of interest. I can visit a Rembrandt painting and know intuition awaits me.

A: Where I would not find intuition there. If I were to look at a poem by Wallace Stevens, however, I would almost be guaranteed some intuitional experience.

D: That leaves us with a question. Can intuition be worked or pursued? Consciousness continues to compute emotional sequences relevant to our lives throughout our lives. These may follow our individual experience, as in Mobius' case, or follow experiences foreign to us that we simply need to know about. Consciousness rings the interest bell for self-consciousness enough for self-consciousness to be aware that a game is afoot and intuition may occur. **Its duration is unpredictable. Nor can I rationally compute an intuition. Still, there must be some way in which one can have some control over the process.**

A: So we have the key to understanding the structure of transcendence but it remains forever too complicated to predict or control. But didn't we say that intuition is the heart of creativity?

D: Absolutely, and some creators seem to exercise some control over the intuitive process. They certainly do not command the process or control it rationally, but some artists seem to have access to creativity in a way that many of us do not.

A: So there may be a way in which the self-conscious mind can become creative?

D: Yes. The word 'access' is sounding a bell. One wouldn't necessarily have to control this process if one could find a way to access it. We need some way to get our intuitional process up and running.

A: It is always up and running in consciousness. **Consciousness is an intuition computer.**

D: Agreed, but I am thinking in terms of methodology. Self-consciousness may be able to devise a number of ways to harvest the fruit of consciousness. Isn't this what our dialogues are really about?

A: If that is true, then we must look at creativity as experienced and leave the rational domain altogether. This cannot be analyzed.

D: I think that your words describe our task. We must look at creativity as a process. I will also be curious to see what role language and particularly dialogue play in this whole enterprise.

A: **Can the Socratic Boogie take us inside the creative act? Is it too much to assume that there may be a way to become intentionally creative?**

D: We just keep building those castles in the air, don't we?

A: I think I hear the distant knell of a new dialogue presencing itself. **We really do have to create creativity, don't we?**

D: Let me get my other toga out of the dryer. This is one Boogie I don't want to miss.

~ CHAPTER V ~

Creativity: Intentional Intuition

Anno: Rational control of intuition is no longer an issue; intuition is inherently not rational. Intuition is a series-form thinking that we can not think fast enough to self-consciously compute.

Domini: Yet we spoke of a self-conscious interaction with consciousness. We noted that self-consciousness, as the home of language, has both an emotional awareness and emotional language. There would seem to be ways of intending intuition that we might access.

A: But not control.

D: Language is the problem. **You and I have been intentionally creating intuitions for years. What is it that we do?**

A: **The problem is that we are on sacred ground. Most people think intuition is an occasional accident, and here we are talking about doing it on purpose. Heresy!**

D: I think I can set the record straight. We have described consciousness as an emotional computer whose goal is intuitions. It is somewhat autonomous in its dynamic, but it has an interface with self-consciousness that would appear to give us access to it.

A: So the central task is to establish how we will self-consciously use language to access consciousness.

D: Will being able to access intuition make me creative?

A: Creators develop a system for handling and showcasing intuition, but intuition is their stock and trade. To live life creatively or to find a media in which to express one's creativity is a matter of individual personal choice combined with the effort one is willing to make to find how to use one's intuitions. One develops a style of expression.

D: First and foremost, however, the creator must be able to access his intuitions.

A: And our standing assumption is that everyone can do this, not just a few souls favored by the gods.

D: Everyone has to create their lives through consciousness anyway. We could not have human experience without consciousness' intuition. But, yes, everyone can also self-consciously access their intuition.

A: Enough of this. Let's open the doors. Shall we talk the silence method or the color/tempo method first?

D: No one knows what that means.

A: That was for you. Let's do silence. I use that more than the other.

D: OK. We have said that self-conscious rationality can push conscious emotional intrusions away from it. Self-consciousness can suppress emotionality over and over. The only place where it has no choice is when a survival emergency intrudes and must be attended to. The main point is that when the intrusion is significant and invitational rather than necessary, self-consciousness can turn it down.

A: And these invitations represent two sides of the same coin. They are attractive invitations to journey to new meaning and new significance. They are the road to beauty within the self.

D: But they also represent acquiescence to an emotional adventure whose outcome is unknown. They are a loss of rational control by self-consciousness. The more rational the person, the more likely he is to fear this kind of adventure. These invitations are the road to continually becoming a new person, but that means allowing the old person to disintegrate.

A: And this is our situation in the contemporary world. Our mostly analytic education emphasizes control, not creativity. It is difficult to express, but what we are saying is that there would be no opposition to this kind of intuitional adventure if our rationality had not created an opposition between reason and emotion. There is no natural antipathy of this sort within the self.

D: But the rational perspective has begun to believe in controlled creativity, as if you could create a significant poem or painting without a journey and without changing the person you are.

A: So, in effect, rationality has inadvertently taught us to stifle our own creative growth.

D: But you can never learn too much.

A: Well, many people feel that understanding too much emotionally is painful.

D: Because they are forced to get rid of some useless rigid part of themselves and grow some more. I shouldn't make light of this. Our assumption is different. If you can intentionally create, you can continually out-create the mishaps of painful change.

A: Because you are no longer passive to emotional growth. You are able to let creativity rather than pain have the final word in your self-transformation.

D: Exactly. And having a perspective that embraces self-creativity, I can only pity those who believe that psychology is primarily rational. When Wittgenstein said that psychology was without conceptual foundations, he should have yelled it from the rooftops. Psychology simply cannot succeed in rationally taking over a-rational mental processes like creativity. So let's look at an altogether different basis for living, the creative mind purposely used and itself created.

A: Your choice of phrase is interesting. How many people assume they can create the structures of their own mental processes? Not many. And the few who do probably try it rationally and do not have access to their own creativity.

D: Enough! Let's go to 'silence'. Much of language is rational in the way we use it. We keep ourselves functional, organized, purposive, and intentional. That's the modern life. We have continued to insist that consciousness constantly intrudes on our self-conscious awareness by issuing new invitations or showing us new significance. And generally we suppress most of these. Free associative consciousness winds up emerging only in day and night dreams. How can we give it greater freedom to intrude?

A: One has to first believe this is possible and want to do so.

D: Granted, but how does one make oneself aware of these invitations?

A: Attitudinally, by wanting them.

D: Don't draw it out to much. What does one *do*?

A: One self-consciously finds a place to be with no tasks and no distractions.

D: Yes, but the self-conscious mind will still be racing along computing this year's taxes and making grocery lists. So just being in a quiet place won't do it.

A: Agreed. The most important task is to suppress speech altogether.

D: Take a vow of silence.

A: Not just external speech but mental speech as well. In ten seconds or so you and I from long practice can suppress mental dialogue and listen.

D: Because otherwise self-consciousness would just continue its monologue. So in order to reach the emotional creative system, we silence self-consciousness.

A: Sounds too simple and not nearly dramatic enough.

D: What is dramatic is what happens. One's awareness begins to be flooded with what appears to be random emotion and imagery.

A: And this is not random. These are points of interest. They are moving patterns that have been recognized by consciousness and brought forward into awareness.

D: Because when one's mind becomes silent by suppressing speech, a process of looking and listening immediately begins to presence itself. One is watching the raw stream of consciousness flowing by.

A: The next thing one notices is that some images and some emotional configurations are repeating themselves. The more these images repeat and alter themselves, the more apparent it becomes that these repeaters have a greater potential for significance. They continually generate new aspects of emotional awareness as they continue to mutate.

D: In other words, the repeating images point to centers of interest. And centers of interest are what we are calling invitations.

A: So what does one do? One follows one's inclination and chooses the imagery that seems most compelling. One need not know why it is interesting or why consciousness picked this imagery. The answers to these questions are all future. One need only know that a particular image configuration is interesting.

D: In choosing one of these flowing configurations, one is accepting the invitation to watch it mutate, to allow the whole recombinant imagistic process to take one on its journey.

A: And let us be clear. At this point self-consciousness is doing what it seldom does. It has become a passive spectator to the events of consciousness. It is watching consciousness 'speak', hearing it move through its sensory evolution. It is allowing the constant mutative motion of consciousness free rein to do what it chooses to do.

D: And most importantly, the moment self-consciousness intervenes with the idea of controlling this process, it disappears. Consciousness yields to self-conscious linguistic control and vanishes. This emotional flow, which appeared because there were no words, continues only as long as it is free to move. Words reify the process and turn it to stone.

A: How long does one allow this journey to go on? When is it finished?

D: Take what we learned about intuition and apply it here. One cannot know or predict the length of the journey ending in new significance made manifest. The journey is arbitrary, dependent on one's attention span and just how complex an intuition emerges. Intense significance might emerge in an hour or so and provide the basis for a poem. It might take years and a new philosophy or a new way of life emerges. This does not even need to be a continuous process, this silencing and watching. One can continue to revisit conscious activity again and again, with self-consciousness intermittently leaving the process to take care of its world. The longer journeys show up as repeated interest in the same consuming imagery. The duration until intuitional satisfaction is reached can neither be predicted nor controlled.

A: But what else can self-consciousness do but spectate? Can it be active in any way?

D: One must understand what is critical here before discussing any active role self-consciousness might have. What is critical to the conscious flow is that it must not be stopped. Arresting its motion linguistically causes what one is watching to vanish. The journey is over.

A: So what does one do? Watch until the movie is over?

D: Did you ever ride a horse?

A: Sure. A couple of times, anyway.

D: Did you teach the horse how to run with you on his back, how to maneuver, when to trot and when to gallop?

A: Well, I had reins in my hands to change his direction now and then, but he mostly did what horses do—be a horse.

D: So you would definitely say that as the rider you mostly let the horse do what he already knew how to do: trot, canter, gallop, pee, and so on?

A: Well I certainly did not teach him those things. I guess I depended on the fact that he knew how to do all those things. Where is this going?

D: But you did influence his movement with the reins?

A: Yes, a little gee, a little haw, a little faster or slower.

D: And when you brought him to a dead stop?

A: The ride was over. I got off as best I could.

D: Say that horse is consciousness. He already knows how to do what he does best: run. Say you are self-consciousness. You influence the horse, change his direction a little, suggest that he do this instead of that. But you don't take over and stop him and do it yourself.

A: No, then I wouldn't need a horse. I concur. I basically let him do what he does best.

D: So, too, with consciousness and self-consciousness. I can find my invitation in the way the horse moves and where he wants to go. With self-consciousness, I can intrude associated images and feelings to see if they help the journey. I am suggesting, not commanding. The minute I pull back on the self-conscious reins, the ride is over.

A: Sounds like a skill.

D: One gets better and better at it. Curiosity generally invites you to feed into the imagistic motion. What is happening here? Will that image affect the journey? Does this feeling play any part? Why did that face show up? Who is that person?

A: So you are both listening and responding. With words?

D: Occasionally. Word-images. Mostly emotional phrasing. Rigid syntax is control power and stops the motion.

A: So to be maximally trite, you all but give the horse 'free rein' and hope that when you minimally intrude on his freedom, he'll think nothing of it and take the suggestion as if he thought of it himself.

D: Somewhat. 'Thought' is too much the property of self-consciousness. When watching and listening to the imagery flow, you need a very light hand. It is, in the last analysis, dialogical. You can tell when you and I talk whether we are helping the flow or obstructing it, or whether a slowing down of the flow is caused by the enigmatic quality of the imagery itself or something you superimposed by introducing conflictive images.

A: That's true. So taking the journey toward intuition is becoming the lesser partner in the dialogue.

D: No. Partners should be equal. Both self-consciousness and consciousness begin minimally. As the journey is prolonged, it involves more motion and imagery. It takes shape more and more. You find yourself contributing more. It's still mostly non-verbal, but you feel or 'intuit' your way better as the dialogue progresses. It cannot be a power trip for either party.

A: Until you can just take over, right?

D: Thanks for being the straight man. NO. You do not want to leave your passive-minimally active stance until the flow completes itself and dramatically pauses. The pause is what we usually experience as conscious intrusion of significance, except in this process you are already there waiting for it. It has product and gets your attention: 'This is important". The difference is that when you pursue and help manage this process intentionally and self-consciously, you are already a partner when the intuition arrives. You have helped bring it to climax.

A: You make it sound like making love.

D: It is every bit of that.

A: But it still sounds abstract. Can you sit and work an example and talk it as you go?

D: I have enough experience to talk it without stopping the flow. OK. Let me suppress speech and see what is happening.

A: I am not in the dialogue from here on, right?

D: True. This will be self-conscious to conscious dialogue, intimate to me and peculiar to my experience. It's *my* flow. OK. Going silent now.

D: Several pictures. One of a moth caught in a spider web. Another of a woman and child I saw on the bus the other day. Another of chasing butterflies in a field. Another of Nefertiti, that famous statuette, its serenity. The bus woman is black. Another of a near accident on the beltway. Coming back to the woman on the bus. She praises her child in English and scolds him in French. Enigmatic. She even looks like the Nefertiti. The interest here is growing. Is it her face? No, something about the space around her. Serenity. She includes the world around her. Her presence is very inviting. I keep watching her and the child. We are all strangers except her. SHE IS AT HOME. OK. First intuition. How do I know she is at home? Am I the stranger? She makes me feel at home. Let it keep unraveling. It is not the child. I have seen her alone. The same quality is there, but what is it? Is she very familiar with her surroundings? No, no more than I. She is simply at home. What does that mean? At home like I was a child chasing butterflies in a field. Images are linking up. Don't want to talk to her. Why not? Just want to watch. Why? Her movements are unhurried and graceful. Can't imagine her anxious. She is very accessible and inviting, open to everything. She is an opening to home. She carries it with her. I want this home for me. She stops my frenetic pace totally. Not as a mother or a woman. It's not there. Simply as the person she is. Puzzling. Why the interest? How does she take home with her? She is never, never a stranger. How? She listens. She is in DIALOGUE with everything around her. How rare. Second intuition. Let me stop here. **She is a moving felt dialogue, which is a home of sorts.**

A: That should help to put some flesh on the bones. I notice you said " first intuition" and "second intuition". What was that?

D: Each one was a breakthrough in my particular image world, insight as to why I was intrigued with the woman. As different imagery flowed it began to return to her repeatedly in different postures and guises. The first journey led me to 'home', the second to 'dialogue as home'. This could have continued and opened out into a great many directions.

A: Now, could you relive or repeat that journey in a medium as a work of art, or is the meaning only personal to your life?

D: Either. Depending on the medium, I would need to shape it some more to showcase my journey. I could paint it, but I am more of a poet, so this journey would most likely become a poem. **Regardless of the medium of expression, all journeys are linguistic and imagistic.**

A: Doesn't this creative journey usually become a work of art?

D: Not necessarily. These two intuitions around this woman have definitely taken me to a new place within myself. Connecting 'home' to 'dialogue' is intriguing to me and compelling. I will now have to self-consciously determine in what way these intuitions are significant to me. I must re-relate the intuitions to who I was, because my sense of myself and my perspective on my experience are different. I feel different. To go on to create a poem would be icing on the cake. Still, I might understand the intuitions better if I wrote the poem. One never knows.

A: I like it. Not surprising that you wound up at dialogue. Not with all our emphasis on it.

D: Intuitions are somewhat parallel to self-conscious interests, but not always. In this case I might add that my sense of dialogue feels richer and different than it was. Somehow I can feel it more deeply from both sides and both people.

A: So you suppressed mental speech, watched images mutate, added some imagery of your own, and wound up taking not one but two journeys. That's a brief summary. And I can do this whenever I want to.

D: Suppose you don't want to. I mean, suppose you are not in the mood.

A: Slick. You are taking us to the color/tempo method.

D:Are we done here?

A: Almost. You noted a couple of intuitions within your journey. How could you tell that they were intuitions? I didn't make the same associations you did.

D: Yes, that needs emphasizing. You wouldn't make the same associations I did. Each person's experiential emotional sensorium is different. In each intuition the sense of the presence of the imagery heightened considerably. The sense of insight and re-orientation of myself emotionally were factors. Things had linked together for me that were previously not associated in any dramatic way. The intuitions each momentarily stopped my self-conscious watching and speaking. Stopped them.

A: But linking or associating imagery is something we do self-consciously all the time. What makes your experience any different?

D: Because I was not analytically comparing experience or emotion. I was expanding the presence of the flow of imagery, not reducing it. I was following the motion of my consciousness and dialoguing with it. Its path surprises me, but, more importantly, it pauses or stops in places that are very significant and new to me. There is no questioning the notion that the surprise *happens to me.*

A: So it is like Mobius following the twist in his belt without knowing why, but needing to see where it goes. Of course, where it went blew his mind.

D: The intuitions I discovered were not that powerful, but they might have been. Mine were small 'Aha's', not big ones.

A: Our whole dialogue is a big one, yes?

D: It's certainly looking that way. On to tempo/color. What manner of beast slouches toward our dialogue to be born?

A: We can do this on purpose, this intuiting, right?

D: YES! ... OK. Can't say it too often. We suppress speech and follow consciousness to its intuitive conclusions. We get better at using our self-conscious minds to input imagery along the journey. We also get better at making the transition from intuitional bursts of significance to their linguistic translations. From there we use our analytic skills to determine the empirical relevance of these intuitions to our experi-

ence and the world. We abstract, compare, create structure and slow down the imagery. Now, can we go on?

A: And all this is tantamount to a methodology for being intentionally creative, a methodology that uses our mental processes in the way they were meant to be used.

D: Yes. Absolutely. Anytime. Anywhere. On purpose. Unless you don't feel like doing it.

A: But that happens all too frequently. Can't you arbitrarily change the way you feel about wanting to create?

D: Let me feed you now. You have more experience here. You are asking if there is a legitimate way to travel through emotion under self-conscious direction in order to get to the emotion that wants to create and transcend.

A: To want to 'Aha', to want to surge forward into unknown territory, to want the intense presencing of beauty—I am saying this is its own emotion. One recognizes the place where one is interested without knowing why, when one knows an invitation is presencing itself. One knows how it feels to not be able to look and listen intensely enough.

D: But is one passive to this emotion? Does one wait on the corner for it like a bus?

A: Like all emotions it is a cluster of sensations: curiosity, welcome, excitement, heightened anticipation of a reward. Until you feel it, you cannot do it.

D: I can't command myself to go there and create?

A: You cannot command a horse to tap dance. He does what he does best, no more, no less. You can only shape the way he does it.

D: What I am asking is can you mutate yourself emotionally from anger because the car won't start to wanting to create? Can you intentionally do this?

A: Too big a jump all at once, but shaping emotion without blocking or stopping it is a skill that can be acquired. It is something like what you do when you follow and interact with consciousness, only this shaping has a specific emotional trajectory and goal.

D: You talk it. This is your best skill.

A: OK. Let me see…Hmmm. Everyone can intersubjectively talk emotion and talk about emotion, because many of the associations attached to each emotion are experientially the same, and have the same language names. We could get into a difficult rational discussion concerning whether you and I mean the same thing when we use the word 'pain', but this is not necessary. We aren't going to do this rationally anyway. All we need to know is that even if our associations vary across any given emotion, we share enough to talk. Add to this that the emotional system is not one of exactness but one of constantly refining approximations and we have a starting place. Each of us needs a method for moving from one emotion to another that works for him or her.

D: OK, but emotions are already moving. So this becomes a task of moving what is already moving. I must move across something that is moving.

A: Just so. I liken it to riding my horse along with a bunch of other horses. Horses are emotions. I must acquire the skill to move from my horse's back to the back or backs of other horses while we are all galloping.

D: It sounds like a circus trick. This is very difficult, yes?

A: That wasn't the intention. It reinforces the concept that I am in motion as well as the horses. I, who am in motion myself, must direct my movement while they are moving.

D: I am not sure that was any better. The horses are the emotions you wish to ride?

A: And I may have to switch horses several times to get to the horse I want.

D: This is getting too abstruse. How do you *do* it?

A: You have to find a way to classify the way emotions are and the way they move, a way that tells you quickly both where you are and where you want to go. My tempo/color schemata is not that original although it works fine for me. It is a system that basically gives me a quick fix on the speed and texture of a given emotion.

D: So when you travel emotionally, you must know from where to where, correct?

A: Yes. **I classify emotions in three ways. The first is tempo.** Anger is a fast emotion. Happiness, too, moves well but not as fast as anger. Contentment, related to happiness, moves fairly slowly. I need to know how great a speed change is involved in moving from one emotion to another.

D: So you are comparing motion to motion. What about, say, sadness?

A: As you might expect, very slow. Most passive emotions are very slow, except for fear, and I call them feelings to distinguish them from emotions. Emotions, which, as the word indicates, move out, are active projections, and move fairly quickly.

D: **OK, go to temperature.** That is the second, is it not?

A: I use a hot/ cold spectrum on emotion. This combines well with tempo. Anger is quick and hot. Joy is quick moving but lukewarm. Remember these classifications serve me personally. Your fix on these emotions might differ slightly from mine, which is fine. Both speed and temperature tell me how far away from each other two emotions are. This is a degree of difficulty rating. Changing speeds from very slow to very fast or changing temperature from very hot to very cold takes a lot of work. If it takes too much work, the question is whether it is worth it. I'll return to this point later.

D: Yes, postpone that until you include color. Why do you need color?

A: It's an old classification and it is useful to me. Color is probably where many emotions got their names. Take anger again. Anger is a deep red, always. Fear is bluish gray-black, depending on the kind of fear and its speed. Hatred is a dark blue-black. Hope is pink and yellow, rainbow-ish. Basically, the more intensely the emotion presences, the deeper its color. Again, my choice of colors is not nor need it be yours. Through practice, I can identify emotions fairly quickly using my three-fold quick fix. I know emotions occur in clusters, so this is not a purity exercise. I just ballpark the dominant emotions.

D: I see. So anger is fast, hot, and red for you. What does that tell you?

A: It tells me it is a fast horse, meaning if I am feeling angry, I can move to another fast emotion with a great deal more facility than I can move to a very slow one.

D: So you are classifying emotion so you can intentionally move across it. You are classifying emotion to map its motion and texture. What is the goal? To move from an emotion that is not serving you to one that is?

A: **Exactly.** And the movement is usually not all at once unless I start out feeling close to where I want to go. Usually I have to ride several emotions to get where I want to go. By the way, this is an exceptional amount of work, and I do not recommend it except in special cases.

To get to the emotion that desires transcendence and beauty is one of those special cases.

D: So you classify where you are—say, angry—and where you want to go—say feeling happy—and you assess the difference between them?

A: Yes. The classification gives me a general problem set. If I am very angry, feeling happy is very remote. My anger is very present, the happiness feeling far away. Feeling happy is a paler red, not as intense as anger, but still red. And happy is a good bit slower than anger and somewhat cooler. Anger to happiness, then, is not as great a journey as one might initially think.

D: Does emotion have a center?

A: After fear is superceded, the central emotion is love. It is red spectrum, rhythmically pleasing, and body temperature, neither warm nor cold. It is the reference point for all the other emotions.

D: It seems that love would be emotionally close to the creative feeling.

A: Very close. To enter the self-dialogue journey towards intuition and beauty requires self-love, or lovingness. Its cluster includes hope, acceptance, forgiveness, mercy, joy, exaltation—all very complex but accessible.

D: All right. So you do your classification and you find you want to move from anger to happiness. How do you actually control this interior movement?

A: 'Control' is too strong. Go back to the horse analogy. I ride the horse. The minute I think I intimately control what the horse is doing, I fail. I ride emotion, not control it.

D: OK. Semantics. What do you actually do?

A: The way one feels at any given moment may be described as what is present to one at that moment. It may be present because of ongoing events, or memories, or even because of mental dialogue. Heidegger is my teacher here. It is best to look at self-consciousness here in terms of what is present to it—as well as what is absent from it. The awareness must be kept temporal to understand it. What is present to me, in my face, is how I feel. What is not present to me is absent; this is how I do not feel. And what is present or absent is constantly moving, mutating and mixing.

D: I'll say it one more time. What do you *do*?

A: I presence or absence, or, more specifically, I presence one emotion to absence another. Language is the great sea in which all emotions can be located. Didn't you ever desire to be happy and begin by recalling happy events from your memories?

D: Sure, but that only works a little. Where are you going?

A: Surprisingly, you can get better at presencing an emotion with practice. **If I want to presence a happy image, I don't just recall a snapshot of it. I revisit it, continuing to call up textures and images that contributed to that happiness. And I don't just remember these details.** I make them as sensorily concrete as possible. I don't just remember

110

that day my daughter opened her Christmas present, but that her hair was flopping around, and she had on her funny Christmas morning bedroom slippers, and that she carefully removed the ribbon and then tore the wrapping paper to shreds in her eagerness. As the details get more specific, concrete and sensual, the event ceases to be a memory and becomes present, a presence.

D: Seems complex. The more present you make the chosen event, the more you 'absent' the emotion you were feeling when you started. I see you switching horses, or more properly, switching presences.

A: You're getting there, but other factors come into play. Learning to presence well is essential. I've had groups of people try this and some very rational types cannot do it at all. With practice maybe. This is wholly within the emotional system but under rational direction. Do you see?

D: Yes. Presencing a past event requires that image and language be carefully invoked and evoked until you get there and are present in it. I suppose then it fills your consciousness.

A: Just so. On to other factors. If I am very angry, how difficult is it to presence the joy of my daughter's opening of her Christmas present?

D: They seem to be quite an emotional distance apart, don't they? I don't think I could do that. Now if I were sitting in front of the fireplace feeling mellow, it would be a piece of cake.

A: And that in a nutshell is the whole problem of movement across emotion. Big leaps may be impossible, but why couldn't incremental presencings achieve the same end?

D: You mean it isn't just finding the correct single counter-image to presence. You may have to move through several presencings to get where you are going.

A: You've got it. And is that always emotionally worth it? This is emotional work, whatever else you would like to call it. I try to move within fairly congruent emotions, but I need my system to tell me what emotions are congruent. Anger to happiness is slowing down, decreasing intensity and heat, and is surprisingly doable. I believe this is what Heidegger meant by "poetic thinking", a continuous series of presencings leading to an emotional result.

D: You took off again. Talk about the other problems.

A: **Well, images as well as memories wear out. By that I mean that each time you re-presence a memory or image, it becomes more difficult to do so.** It isn't true that you can maintain the vivacity of a given image. **So you have to continue coming up with new images to presence.** It is not an insuperable problem, but it is something to remember when you invest your emotional energy in this kind of traveling.

D: Makes sense. Aren't some memories so powerful that they can be used over and over?

A: Yes, especially ones you initially helped to create. Images of your own successful art, poems, paintings, successful furniture creations—

all serve as places that can be presenced repeatedly. In general, the more your life is characterized by creative understandings you have undertaken, the more material is at your disposal for presencing.

D: So give me an actual sequence. Let me see it work.

A: Say I am angry. My car won't start. I have some spare time to myself and I decide to journey, but I don't feel like it. Mentally I know what I want, but I cannot journey in anger. Say I first presence something exciting but not angry. Same speed, different emotion. Maybe taking off in a big jet plane. Exciting. Then I see if I can slow anger down. I pick something irritating. Let's see. OK. I presence salt from snow plows all over the windshield of my car, and how I feel. Yeah, it happens, it's irritating, but it's no big thing. The anger cools off a little. Then maybe I sequence irritation with a success, something upbeat. OK. I do woodwork. I made a nice desk, but when it was finished I saw a crack running down the side. Irritating, because as time passed the crack was going to open up. Then I remembered that I had already seen the crack and glued it before I finished the desk. Satisfaction behind irritation. So I am now a little anticipatory and excited, not overwhelmed by anger anymore, and have a recent presenced sense of success. I've opened up my receptivity. I am ready to travel. I then further presence the desk, since it is still on my mind. I want more of the sense of creating and designing it, the feeling of that, and of making and finishing it and enjoying the final product. I am now presencing a past journey. I am finally ready to suppress speech, listen and start a new journey. I was angry. It has been absenced, displaced, and vanished. In its place is presenced 'waiting for an invitation'. The new dynamic is fairly fast but not as fast as anger, and it is not nearly as intense. I am not now passive, either. I am in a different 'good place'. It took four or five horses, but I am there.

D: But why not just jump from anger to your feeling of making the desk and wanting to create it? Why take little jumps?

A: Sometimes you get lucky and one jump does it. It's best to take a look at how big the jump is in terms of the change needed. How 'far away' is it to where you want to go? How slow to how fast? How hot to how cold? What color to what other color? From real anger to creative readiness? Four or five jumps.

D: What emotion is farthest away from creative readiness?

A: Hatred. Dead cold, dead slow, and a dark blue black.

D: Would you be able to make that transition?

A: Too many jumps. I wouldn't even want to, would I?

D: No, I guess not. Your enacted transition sequence was believable to me. Was that a real sequence you talked?

A: You bet. My car won't start and I was angry.

D: I know you talked it but did you really do it?

A: Very much so. Having this dialogue as an ongoing environment allows me to presence the creative inclination faster than I normally could, so I did not quite start from scratch. Yes, I performed the presencing motions that absenced my anger and took me to the place where I want to create.

D: So you can move to the intuitive journey anytime you want to, almost regardless of where you start from?

A: Thanks for appreciating this method, but mostly it represents the long way around. The best sense I have of it is that presencing is a good anchor. I know that if all else fails that the presencing activity can get me there. I also think that there is a much more normal way for that to happen.

D: I follow you. There is always a lot of conscious intrusion into self-consciousness, feelings and imagery that say 'Pay attention. This could be important to you.' If you simply cultivate the habit of listening for these, the invitational opportunities increase tenfold.

A: My thoughts exactly. If I can remember to stop talking at myself most of the time and spend some time listening and musing, the invitations show up.

D: And for the rationalist or control freak, this would be a waste of time.

A: Because the listening represents the beginnings of dialogue. Dialogue is *listening* and talking. The rationalist wants a monologue.

D: Back to our twofold method. I find that the ability to intend to create and the capacity to purposively succeed in this intention give me a confidence in the whole process of creating that I would not otherwise have.

A: It's the difference between blind groping, hoping something shows up, versus knowing one has the ability to move over and in to the place one desires to go to. I know one way or the other I have gotten there and can always get there.

D: Because we are using our mind the way it uses itself. I said that wrong. We are self-consciously reinforcing the way the mind already works, and we can alternate between creativity and reason as the need arises.

A: Yes. I don't think the freedom that results from co-opting one's own mind as it operates should be underestimated. The more you increase access to your own mental activity, the more you possess potential options to participate in your own creation.

D: Does this signify that we human beings prefer to be fishes, to be in motion, to be animistic? I don't think that's true.

A: No, human beings are not going to return to their pre-rational existence. The future lies in having both reason and creativity at one's disposal. They are, after all, a functioning unit.

D: We do not live in a very creative age.

A: That is why we are talking. Reason dominates creativity overmuch. A new balance has to be achieved. If one doesn't create, what new experience is there to be reasoned? I simply can't be satisfied with having rigid control over the vicissitudes of my fast-paced modern life. And if pleasure is the real goal, why, taking a journey into intensely presenced beauty tops a cold beer or money in the bank every time. Our age has to learn to be creative.

D: Agreed. It is high time. Do you think the multifaceted psychiatric problems of our age derive from a lack of emotional creativity?

A: The speed and complexity of our lives force us to be more rationally organized. To live in or near a city requires organization of one's time and effectiveness in one's personal habits. Still, if everyone is emotionally breaking down, it is obvious that we cannot afford to be continuously rational at the expense of being emotionally creative.

D: And if people used these creative methods, they would paradoxically have more control over their creativity.

A: Well, you are really touching on another discussion. We have been discussing creativity as if its purpose was to create art or new ideas to support our technology, but creativity's main purpose is to create our own mental process.

D: That is another discussion, something under a heading such as 'Thinking Makes It So'. What I think I am using to arrange the world controls how I actually do it.

A: Yes. Our images of our mind are assumptions about what minds do. Everyone has a different set of assumptions and therefore creates a different product. Psychiatrically speaking, we live in an age that calls for the intentional creation of the mind.

D: Mind is simply a complex image. It can be accessed.

A: That better be true, or one is stuck with one's assumptions.

D: Haven't we been creating our minds in this dialogue?

A: Generally to some extent, but creating the mind is a specific task. Let's talk about it later.

D: Good. I am tired.

A: Muscle tired? Is your mind a muscle? Can you wear it out like a machine? What is "tired"?

D: "Tired" is 'Give it a rest'. Until we talk again. Capisce?

A: You just ran out of gas, right?

D: I AM NOT A CAR!

A: Kidding. Catch you later....

~ CHAPTER VI ~

I Am I; Who Is Me?

Anno: I am still not sure I want to have this dialogue. It is going to be full of double entendres and puns.

Domini: Well, the funniest thing about thinking is that it is not humorous, if you take your thinking seriously.

A: I like that. True humor is a form of intuitional transcendence, moving past the world one was stuck in moments ago.

D: How formal we are! Relax. The most important reason for this dialogue is to explore what our mental processes are really set up to do. To take a look at the limits of our capacities.

A: I thought that is what we have been doing. We have built a marvelous construction that lets us use our mental processes to their best advantage.

D: And people will say that it's not for them. They have their own methods for using their minds. People think their mind and the use of it was given to them. They think that the way they use it is written in stone. How can our dialogues help if people do not know that they had an active hand in creating their own minds?

A: Education would take care of that. Sixteen years of analytical training would crush anyone's creativity. Give me equal time during those sixteen years and I will teach them to be intentionally creative. What a formidable society we could be!

D: Well, you are going to have to start by helping kids and their parents to understand that the assumptions that they make about what a mind is controls how they use it.

A: That's what education is about.

D: Not currently. When were you ever in a classroom where the teacher cautioned that there are no mind facts, that everyone assumes what the mind is? Science and psychology and ethics are supposed to take care of this situation, but they do not. People will and do make assumptions about their mind, and some of these are very harmful.

A: People generally assume that the whole process was just handed to them and the trick is to make the best of it.

D: We need a dialogue to determine why this is so. We are not selling a system to people who don't think they have one. They think they have their own system and that they pretty much know how it works.

A: So you want leverage over their minds, some way to intravenously inject your understanding.

D: Sounds like me, but that would not be a dialogue.

A: I am sorry. I am a little discouraged. Underneath the problem we are tossing around is a larger one. I am still not even provisionally clear on the purpose of mental activity historically, in the long run. To not understand where all this is going, the telos, the end purpose, raises too many questions.

D: So we create a model. Let's think it.

A: And ten years down the road, a new and better model shows up.

D: What is wrong with that? Humanity keeps creating itself. Maybe that is the model.

A: I am starting to get your drift. Suppose I suggest that human mental processes have an unlimited capacity to continually remake themselves from the foundations on up?

D: That's a start. There seem to be obvious potentials in the mind that we do not even use.

A: The *idiot-savant* is a case in point. And what about extrasensory capabilities? What about the future of neurosurgery and enhanced brains? There is no limit.

D: It would be nice to access a computer in our head other than consciousness, just for computational purposes. It would be nice to heal injury to ourselves by using our minds. It would be nice to be telepathic. If you look back at mankind's history, however, you will see that human beings create new mental capacities only as they are needed.

A: I see what you mean. The 'Wouldn't it be nice' scenario lacks drive. Still, it is often true in the modern world that a number of groups around the world attempt to solve the same problem at the same time. Look at the work on super-fast conductors. I concede that historical timing is involved, but it still seems that the future is a blank slate.

D: Like the future of a creative act.

A: Now I hear you. You are looking at mental processing as a creative engine whose function is to continue to create itself from the ground up. It has resources we haven't used yet. And if it lacks the resource, it creates it.

D: Assume we have capacities we will not even look for until we need them. Those certainly aren't predictable. Focus on our current model in which mental processing is a collaboration between creativity and rationality.

A: Yes. Look at the world we have created in only a few centuries.

D: I am more interested in the number of aspects of mind that have been discovered and explored by philosophy and the sciences in the last several generations.

A: Oh. I see. These disciplines have been recreating who the mind is, what it is, and how it is or can be used.

D: And this has greatly changed the way people think their mind works. I have no problem with the evolution of assumptions about the mind. We must make the best assumptions possible. But I will not call them anything more truth-determining than 'assumptions'.

A: What you think is how you think is what you get. There's our dialogue. I want to get at those assumptions. We certainly have ours.

D: You and I, in dialogue, have made assumptions that have allowed us to create a picture of mental processing that will help us alternately create and reason at will. That is a useful set of assumptions.

A: But not hard fact.

D: If the assumptions work, use them.

A: Which appears to be the basis of our understanding of mental processing and the rule for its use.

D: **I want to explore the beneficial and harmful uses of assumption.** P.D. Ouspensky, a twentieth-century philosophical wild man, asserted over and over that analogy is the most effective tool of thought. He acknowledged that not all analogies were serviceable, and that some could be misleading, but he reverenced analogy as a superb tool.

A: And others have taken that up: the mind as simile, as metaphor, as comparison.

D: But analogy lies at the heart of an assumption. 'My mind is like a computer'. This analogical energy is at the heart of mental dialogue and mental processing.

A: That's why I wanted this dialogue. We have built a castle in the air through analogical dialogue. Analogy seems endemic to dialogue. Our castle provides an answer to the question: What is the mind like? We said: "It is like this' or 'It is like that', and created a livable operative understanding. No buildings fell. Traffic did not stop. Simply put, our set of assumptions recreate the mind.

D: Or we used our minds to recreate the mind.

A: Yes, and that seems to be the teleological provisional model. We essentially use our minds to recreate the mind we use.

D: Which makes the assumptions about how the mind is used incredibly important.

A: Exactly. I want to look at why so few people realize that they have made and continue to make those kinds of assumptions all their lives.

D: Because knowing that the way you use your mind is based on assumptions can help you replace them with better assumptions.

A: My thinking, too. Let's begin. What are the major things that influence the formation of the assumptions that people make about how their minds work? This seems to be a very intimate process of awareness, assimilation, and use. Yes?

D: You want to explore the bad to get to the good. Why bother?

A: If people do not know they have made these assumptions, how can they create new ones?

D: An 'assumptive metaphysics'. I kind of like that. We must show in language how these assumptions come to be. And how one determines if they are useful.

A: Assumption is not a creative or rational fault. It is a necessity in mental processing. If so, and we assume it is, it plays a critical role in using the mind. So let's go ahead and take a look at how assumption works. Or at best assume that is what we are doing. I do take my humor seriously.

D: Noted. There are two ways to examine this assumption. Some of our assumptions are based on motions and images in the world that seem analogous to motions in our mind and…

A: We also create emotional pictures of our self-relationship.

D: Let's start with language analogies. Children glean many assumptions about their relationship to their mental processing from the language handed to them, primarily from their parents. These assumptions, rife in language, are in turn derived from thousands of pieces of experiential data. Intersubjective relationship, our mental interaction with others, feeds us images of how the mind works.

A: So we dialogue with others and form images of how our own mind functions. Do some of these images derive from our dialogue with ourselves? I think the notion of some kind of plurality of self is on the table. That would affect our idea of self-communication and the way we come to make assumptions.

D: So let's assume these two avenues. I would like to start with what the world supplies. There are obvious arenas to draw from: sex, war, weather, life cycles, the body and clothing, color and light, and topography. I am not after any kind of exhaustive list. Let's just create some rich content and see what it adds up to. My assumption going in is that all these analogies have both accuracy and usefulness; otherwise we wouldn't use them. Each names a facet of mental processing. What I wish to understand is if the part of existence the analogy was drawn from forces its user to take on the whole process the analogy was drawn from.

A: I am not sure I am following you. Let's take on an example. If I say someone is 'shallow-minded', the analogy compares depth of water to depth of mind. "We are in deep water' means we are in complex circumstances. These are very serviceable images and are good shorthand for observing mental states or motions. They lack a certain rational specificity, but so what. What is it you are looking at?

D: The mind in your analogies is a body of water. Deep water is usually good, but not always, and shallow water is bad. Depth of water equals depth of mind. Does this analogy help overall comprehension of mental activity? The comparison between mind and water is end-stopped and isolated, yet my concern is that the image may spill over (forgive me) into a general understanding of mind at any and all times.

A: In other words, would someone who used these images be forced to create their whole picture of mental processing based on its analogy to a body of water?

D: That's part of it. The other aspect is that these images are accurate, but does their preciseness keep me from looking further into how the whole mind functions?

A: Let's look at some more analogies and see what they have in common. Gender relations are easy. Someone may be 'divorced from reality', 'be married to himself', 'make love to his mind', or even proceed to the violence of 'mind-fucker'.

D: At least these are all about human relationship. They are less spatially and more relationally oriented. Let's go further out.

A: I agree. Let's go to weather and water. A person can 'make waves', have a 'mental storm', feel that an issue is 'cloudy', can 'float on his mind', can feel that his creative energies are 'lying fallow', can 'plough through' an issue, and may possess a 'sea-level mentality'. People take on these images without thinking as they learn the language. How does that hurt anything?

D: That is what I am exploring. All these images connote as well as specify. If I say to someone that his remarks are 'pregnant with meaning', this is both an accurate use of imagery and an implication that the mind is natal or fetal or otherwise involved in gestation.

A: Like 'being born again'. I see the problem. These images all specifically name states or parts of the mind but they are incompatible with each other because they belong to different larger arenas of understanding. Either a person adopts his favorite analogy as his picture of the mind, which is trouble, or he sees mental activity in ten thousand parts with no center.

D: Now we are on the same page. I use hundreds of these images. They do feel accurate but somewhere I know that they are attached to incompatible systems of understanding. When you said at the end of the last dialogue that my thinking just 'ran out of gas', you were jokingly making a point, but think: isn't it dangerous to think of the mind as a mechanical engine? Then we 'take on fuel' and 'go full throttle' and 'get recharged' and may 'take a back seat to someone'. I know what I mean when I use these images, and yet I do not know what I mean.

A: It's as dangerous to think of the mind as a machine as it is to think of human beings as 'intelligent animals'. The overextension of the usefulness of the analogy is at fault here. We are like other animals but actually we are not at all like other animals. We are like machines but not at all like machines, really.

D: That is why all these assumptions bother me. They are certainly part of daily language usage, and I certainly do not want to do away with them, but they are very misleading when used to explain the basis of mental processing.

A: You overstate the problem. These assumptions are merely locators. They point to bits of mental activity, not to the whole. And they do so accurately. Let them be used. They are the particulars of which the whole is constructed. People know what they are.

D: But they differ too greatly to form a whole, and they keep people who use them from seeing the unity of the mind's activity.

A: You forget. People are the unity. They live the unity. They possess it as experienced. I think we may be on the wrong track. People do not build their minds based on this kind of imagery. If they can be said to build their minds, the construction is based on their emotional attitude towards the mind. It is definitely relational more than a question of unifying imagistic particulars. I think there is more gold if we look at how individuals relate to their own minds.

D: Speaking of gold. I can finish this segment now. Each name we give to a particular mental activity we find in our physical experience is a piece of a puzzle. These puzzle pieces increase in quantity daily. The problem is that most of these puzzle pieces belong to different puzzles. Putting them together in one puzzle is impossible.

A: That is a good image to describe the problem.

D: I guess this is what was bothering me. It's probably the language problem. I can illustrate it even better. If one says: 'Shallow-minded people run out of gas quickly', despite one idiom coming from mechanics and the other from water observation, the sentence is perfectly comprehensible because the overarching reference is to the dynamics of mental processing.

A: And somewhere along the line people weave these accurate little pieces into bigger pieces. They do not, however, bother to weave them into a whole, nor could they.

D: A whole such as we are creating. What was bothering me was the conviction that in learning all these idiomatic metaphors people were actually blocking their access to their central mental processing. What I see now is that all these bits and pieces provide new observations on the particulars of minute to minute thinking.

A: That's why the richest thinking is found in new slang.

D: What? Gotcha. Slang names movements of sensation that have no names.

A: I was looking at a computer hacker's dictionary on the web the other day and the imagery simply turned my head around. Listen to some of these images: "teledildonics", "friode", "progasm", "mumblage", "fiber-seeking backhoe", and "ambimousterous". They all describe computer/hacker interactions, and often describe mental processes that do not yet have names. What riches!

D: So the problem is not here. What problem? Why people do not access the centers of their mental processing to a greater extent and are content to simply use whatever they inherit.

A: And let's take a good look at that. **The most powerful aspect of this problem is that the 'I' specifically feels that it is in relationship to another person.** Should I be afraid of my mind?

D: If you are afraid of it you must have assumed that it was something to be feared. Assumptions, here we come!

A: Why must I do battle with my mind?

D: You must have assumed the relationship is adversarial.

A: Can I sneak up on my mind and surprise it?

D: Who assumed one could hide from the mind? You.

A: I have to tightly control the mind or it gets out of hand and gets me into trouble.

D: Did you assume the mind is uncooperative, chaotic, or the enemy? Why did you?

A: I must overpower the mind's resistance to me.

D: You have assumed your mind is fighting you for its life.

A: I must question my mind relentlessly in order to make it give up its secrets.

D: So you assume your mind is someone who may or may not answer, someone who hides.

A: I have no problem lying to my mind. What it doesn't know can't hurt it.

D: Doesn't your mind know everything you do and are? Did you assume your mind was an unforgiving parent?

A: Why does my mind lie to me and confuse me?

131

D: How do you approach your mind? Aren't you welcome? You assume what you want is not there for the asking.

A: It takes all my courage to think.

D: Only if you assume someone is there to exact a penalty if you do not do it right.

A: I am not intelligent enough to understand my mind.

D: Why would you assume intelligence is the foundation of your relationship to your mind?

A: Thinking makes me tired. It is a struggle and an effort.

D: Did you assume great effort was involved in thinking? Or that the mind resists you?

A: I am a slave to my mind. I don't have any power over it.

D: You assumed that the mind is a master who has all the power.

A: Master or not, I do not have the necessary power.

D: Maybe neither of you has any power. Why assume otherwise?

A: I am pragmatic. I treat my mind like a team of oxen. It had better produce results.

D: Or what? You will get a new team of oxen?

A: I love my mind. It embraces everything I am and do.

D: That is because your mind is you.

A: My mind laughs at my attempts to understand.

D: What would it gain by doing that?

A: Sometimes I just have to shut my mind down and do what I want.

D: Why would you discard that kind of help?

A: My mind is an exquisite tool that I use very well.

D: Doesn't it also use you? Why couldn't it be cooperation between equals?

A: My mind is so confused. I can go days without one clear idea.

D: If you don't talk to your mind, how would you know what it was doing?

A: It takes a lot of courage to think. It is dangerous. I could mis-think and wind up a vegetable.

D: You assume an arena of judgment and penalty. Why?

A: I like to ignore my mind the way it ignores me.

D: Ignore someone who loves you? Try talking to each other.

A: I hate it when I am tired and my mind just keeps churning.

D: At least it never quits on you. Do you want it to stop?

A: If I want to be calm, my mind is racing. If I want to think about next week, my mind is occupied with something that happened ten years ago.

D: There is no such thing as one-way cooperation.

A: Nobody really understands anything. Best to just play life as it lays and forget about thinking.

D: That won't stop the conversation. Why not dialogue? What have you got to lose, except your mind?

A: **We have hit the mother lode. It is the relationship people have to themselves that shuts their mental doors.**

D: I think we have shown that. People have been taught that the almighty 'I' stands alone, is responsible and must somehow run its show. This reveals a simple truth to me that not many people have even guessed at.

A: Which is?

D: When you talk to yourself, who do you talk to?

A: I'm with you. I could say I don't really talk, or that I talk to me.

D: Who is 'me'?

A: I always thought it was a head-mechanics thing. 'Me' is everything I have ever been or thought, my past self, a reflexive echo. 'I' am the present and to some extent the future.

D: But we mentioned before that we were convinced that 'me' is listening.

A: We didn't go that far. We decided that when 'I' speaks inside the mind, 'I' is absolutely convinced that someone is listening.

D: Who is listening?

A: Another person, I suppose. I see. How many am I? Am I a 'we'?

D: I do not believe, however interesting it is, that we need to go that far. Within the mind, people don't speak as if they were speaking to a tree. They speak to a person. Suffice it to say that each person is involved in a mental dialogue.

A: Like our dialogue, only the interior experience is more intimate than talking to you.

D: Exactly, and as Gadamer indicates, learning to think is primarily learning the process of dialogue. The ethical dimension of dialogue is not moral. It is aesthetic and creative. The better you learn to create dialogue, the closer you come to complete access to yourself, or, in our case, the other person.

A: And the place you learn to do that is in your head. You learn to talk with other people and they help you learn dialogue, but the most important place you dialogue is in your head. Why don't people know this?

D: The people who spoke to them might have done so in a monologue, issuing orders or threats or challenges or advice. Small wonder some of us grew up talking to ourselves and other people in the same way. Dialogue was never part of their experience.

A: All true, but where I was heading is to observe that we now have a third dialogue within mental processing. **We have one between consciousness and self-consciousness, one between reason and emotion, and now, within self-consciousness, we are speaking of a completely linguistic dialogue apparently taking place between plural selves.** I am getting confused a little.

D: I see what you mean . **I think that the answer is that dialogue in its most interior meaning transcends language. Better if we think of it as intimate interaction that results in communication, verbal or non-verbal. Between consciousness and self-consciousness is a dialogue that is partly pre-verbal and partly verbal.** Between reason and emotion, too, the dialogue seems to transcend the actual interactivity. Communication takes place and we call it dialogue. Within self-consciousness, we have dialogue as conversation in language, which is our most common understanding of the term 'dialogue'.

A: I like this last kind of dialogue and where we have gone with it. I know self-conscious conversation is not overly formal. It is filled with unspoken feelings and images and its syntax is not at all orderly, but, as linguistic dialogue, it forces me toward the notion of a plural 'I', one speaking and one listening.

D: And the plural self may well be the true situation within mental processing. It is the rationalists who have made their stand on the singular 'I'. If the plural self undercuts the autocratic quality of the ego, then I am for it. **Awareness that we dialogue in our head, not monologue, would help to change the many bad self-to-self relationships that we have just looked at.**

A: You had to include 'self-to-self', didn't you. Plural.

D: Why not? It is already, for some reason, in our language. I'd like to see where we are. It seems we are coming full circle. We began a dialogue and soon learned that access to mental process is achieved through dialogue. The term 'dialogue' is taking on a lot of weight.

A: That's what we have been doing. Dialoguing, and placing a lot of weight on it.

D: It's the Socratic Boogie all over again, isn't it?

A: **We are calling three things dialogue. All are intimate to our self-relationship. The relation between reason and emotion, self-consciousness and consciousness, and I and Me.** The 'I' and 'Me' is experienced directly as dialogue, or dualogue, if you wish. The dialogue between reason and emotion is experienced implicitly. Self-consciousness and consciousness are also implicit and we have tried to make the relationship explicit. But the essence of their interaction is what we are calling dialogic.

D: It seems to me the most egregious fault in modern assumptions is that the 'I' is the supreme commanding general of the whole self. We have discussed and discarded that notion in favor of the plural dialogic self. The emphasis has to fall on the interaction between any two centers of mental processing, and not on who is in control.

A: No argument. The minute the relationship is seen as Master/Slave, dialogue is precluded.

D: I do not think dialogue is such a difficult notion to access, but the commanding 'I' has warped this notion altogether. **Too many philosophers have monologued, and inadvertently or purposely given us a picture of the mind as a static command center under the direction of the 'I'.**

A: This is the mind/body dualism of Descartes. **It is the dialogic interaction of the I/Me that defines the self, not the single rational 'I'. Motion defines, not reason.**

D: My thinking, too. We have dialogued to the point of understanding that mental processing is dialogic at its core, both intrinsically between consciousness and self-consciousness and overtly between the 'I' and 'Me'. Nothing dealt with in this dialogic discourse is inside or outside a mind. Our very human existence is, and is experienced as, dialogue. Reason has coerced these relationships into inferior-superior partnerships: reason over primitive emotion, self-conscious command over murky conscious chaos, and the I over the pitiful whine of the Me.

A: But doesn't dialogue imply opposition? Dialectic certainly seems oppositional. Choices do have to get made.

D: I believe that is what we want to set straight. The last four hundred years of ascending rational dominance has absolutized the ego. This movement performs an 'us and them' remaking of mental processing. It has polarized the philosophical pairs, whether the discussion was time/space or quantity/quality. This was not always so. The Greeks understood. The 'dia' in dialogue means across, not against. It implies a back and forth, from one to the other. Opposition is a product of this polarization, a bastardization of the original notion.

A: But within emotion you certainly have a compare-and-contrast movement taking place. Isn't that going to involve opposition?

D: Comparing and contrasting is the mode of thinking we use in all talk. The goal is to make useful distinctions. There a is a large difference between deciding what dominates what over and against deciding which distinctions are more useful. One is a power trip; the other is not.

A: Are you implying that this is simply a question of emphasis? Emphasizing dominance, answers, and ego destroys dialogue, and emphasizing distinction allows it to continue?

D: Yes, and we have returned to self-relationship as the basis of dialogue. **The rational places tremendous weight on expedience: this, NOT that. The emotional mind, which the rational avoids and despises, is always a 'both/and' process, approximating, summarizing, and expanding.** So let us return to the fundamentals of dialogue. I am glad we explored the way in which the modern rational prejudice has imbalanced our thinking processes. We have discovered that the distortions within our mental processing affect not only our I/Me dialogue, but have a very deleterious effect on less well understood relationships, such as the one between consciousness and self-consciousness.

A: The genesis of dialogue is the awareness that something is significant or interesting, and this interest generates an invitation to undertake a journey. This is a very special emotion in its own right. The journey has as its goal the beauty and satisfaction of intuition.

D: And this journey can be pre-conscious or self-consciously observed and experienced. It is a collaboration between consciousness and self-consciousness in which exploration and curiosity dominate.

A: Which is never a rehearsal of the known. Past experience cannot determine the outcome. Something new to the self will emerge.

D: Which is implicit in the act of dialoguing. One does not undertake dialogue to discover what one already knows. The anticipation of a change in self accompanies all such journeys.

A: Are we specifying a journey within the mind or one between two separate people?

D: Both. This exploratory journey can be intrasubjective or intersubjective. The plural self guarantees the similarity of situations.

A: So exactly what controls the mind away from dialogue and toward a power struggle between unequal speakers?

D: As clearly as I can put it, we discovered that assumptions about the nature of human relationships determine both the social posture and the relationship within the mind.

A: So what is emerging is an ethics of self-relationship. The relationship cannot be pedantic, domineering, or competitive. It must be loving, hopeful, without fear, malleable, and responsive. The partners in the dialogue must be deemed equal. Their investment in the dialogue must be equal. Without the understanding that the self is plural, 'I' cannot dialogue with 'Me'.

D: Without the understanding that the self is plural, we must regard it as a static command center. The function of the rational 'I' is to decide, not dialogue. If the self is plural, it is always in motion and in dialogue. The 'I' can also be a dialogue partner.

A: And we discovered that for many people this plural self notion creates immense rational frustration. Motion, as dialogue, is 'out of control'. What is this, they say, 'mind by committee'?

D: Still, lest we forget, science deals successfully with all kinds of motion. Can't rationality handle this motion?

A: Science stands outside that motion entrenched in the observing static 'I'. It must. That is a far cry from being the motion and speaking from within it.

D: The rational mind cannot discover that it is essentially not a thing. We have created the true basis of mental process: it is dialogue. The 'mind' of the rationalist is actually ceaseless cognitive motion.

141

Reason can supercede this motion to achieve its purposes, which are legitimate. The trouble comes specifically at the point where the mind is assumed to be *only* rational.

A: This is too negative. We are assuming that, regardless of the many centuries of rational dominance, Western civilization is gradually paying attention to the emotional with new respect. We are also watching a slow movement that is overcoming its fear of cognitive emotion.

D: If our civilization can accept the emotional system as fundamental and natural and the foundation of interior dialogues. If it can develop respect for the sophistication of that system.

A: Back to dialogue, the two of us talking. I have noticed that we do not insist on what we know, one to the other.

D: Because we know that what we discuss is in flux, and will mutate and evolve. **We ASSUME the journey.**

A: **But do we assume the outcome?**

D: **I think so. We assume we will be changed, and that the change will signify our growth as people.**

A: Dialogue, then, cannot be undertaken assuming a negative outcome.

D: It wouldn't be dialogue if it did. But I hear you. Doesn't dialogue possibly cause suffering? Doesn't all fundamental emotional change involve suffering?

A: We need to be specific here. Some of this 'suffering' is offset by anticipation. If dialogue creates the intuitional journey towards intense presencing, it seems to me that the significance of the outcome, its importance, is already anticipated within the emotional sensorium of the self, even before it is subsequently thought or reasoned.

D; I'll buy that. So if these intuitions require a change in self-definition, one who anticipates this will suffer less pain. But there is still pain in adjusting to the change in self-definition.

A: There has to be. Everyone clings to aspects of themselves in the form of emotional habits. I am saying **that if one conceives oneself fundamentally as change, the adjustment to new understanding is less severe.**

D: But these intuitions will inevitably be a surprise.

A: Yes, but if I am dialogically in motion and suddenly find myself elsewhere than I anticipated, that is a natural state. **Only if I insist on standing still will my discoveries be traumatic.**

D: So the rational assumption concerning the static posture in which one insists on trying to stand still causes the major trauma we are calling 'suffering'.

A: I believe so. The Greeks knew better until Aristotle started us on the long rational journey. Good on, Socrates.

D: Don't make that long journey, which is motion, evolution, alteration, and change toward the rational something negative. The result is now a formidable dialogue between the emotional and the rational, between consciousness and self-consciousness.

A: Is it fair to say that the sheer growth of language specificity created that dialogue?

D: It may be better to see language as less causal and more as itself dialogue, a constantly expanding medium of exchange. In language the rational and the emotional meet and trade. Conscious intrusion of emotion becomes self-conscious rational task. Language creates our latest dialogue, the I/Me dialogue.

A: Why do I continue to have a problem with the intrasubjective dialogue understanding? I keep feeling the need, if the self is plural, to name the dialoguers or otherwise distinguish them.

D: Aren't 'I' and 'Me' sufficient?

A: They probably should be, but in my mental dialogue I swim back and forth so much that I lose track of who talks to whom.

D: That is why I believe our interior dialogues are our model for dialogue. When you lose the self-conscious distinctness of the 'I' while pursuing mental dialogue, your awareness is simply that of ongoing response.

A: That occurs off and on when you and I dialogue. There are sequences when I am not sure who is speaking. But with you and me, all I need do is look across the room to confirm that I am talking to a separate person.

D: That's an advantage and a disadvantage. Which is why your own interior dialogue is the ultimate training ground. **To lose the constant awareness of who talks to whom is to be so thoroughly involved in the path of the journey that who is speaking no longer matters.** This is overwhelmingly analogous to the mystic who must lose his ego to find his true self. One begins dialogue in ego isolation and ends with a plural self merged in dialogue.

A: Dialogue is virtually synonymous with self-transformation.

D: **Since dialogue is the heart of creativity, it not only transforms the self but the world around that self.**

A: All the time we spent creating the mind was simultaneously an exercise in rediscovering and recreating the foundations of dialogue itself.

D: Creating it by doing it, the only way one can learn to do it.

A: We learn about it and we learn ourselves by doing it.

D: Since we are actually dialoguing about dialogue, our awareness is harvesting new understanding about how we understand.

A: Human beings are first and foremost dialogic, expanding and shaping their world.

D: Where all the positives and negatives meet across their usefulness in our lives.

145

A: And the more we dialogue, the more we will transcend the impedimental assumptions that have obstructed our self-understanding, the ones we learned as children.

D: To be philosophically formal, this cognitive motion termed 'dialogue' is the foundation of a position called 'Meontology". We are not, as humans, fundamentally being, a thing, but a motion, a happening, a 'not-yet-being'. As the Bible would have it, we "creatio ex nihilo", create ourselves from 'no-thing'. Interesting theology. As 'imago dei', humans, like God, create themselves and the world 'from nothing', from this dialogic motion within the self.

A: Sounded a little pontifical there. You threw me off.

D: How about 'Life is the celebration that is dialogue'.

A: Which never stops.

D: So what have we learned? That the inhibition to true dialogue has its basis in the many assumptions people make about their self and mind. That these assumptions have their greatest power in not being known to be assumptions.

A: And that dialogue will continually manifest and transcend these assumptions.

D: So where do we go from here?

A: We must move to the future of this understanding. It can remake our contemporary world.

D: Which is still predominantly rational and masculine.

A: Funny you should throw in 'masculine'. I meant to mention that some of our most powerful dialogical understanding emerges from the male-female relationship. We need a dialogue there, too.

D: OK. Two dialogues. I want to go future first. It makes better sense of the past. Where are we going?

A: I am going to bed and let the Socratic Boogie percolate in my dreams.

~ CHAPTER VII ~

Mars and Venus: the Terrae Incognitae

Anno: We cannot leave male-female relationship untouched and project the future of our dialogic enterprise.

Domini: It may be the model for all other dialogues. It is certainly the most overtly skewed relationship in the modern world outside of reason and emotion. Possibly for the same reasons. Or emotions.

A: Yes. The word I was trying to recall this morning was 'androcentric'. We live in a world where what is normal is male. Everything else is deviant or inferior or abnormal.

D: And we live in a world dominated by reason.

A: And one controlled by balances of power.

D: Male, rational, and control by mastery of power.

A: Female, a-rational or emotional, intuitive, and relational. But if our world has male masters it must have female slaves. The imbalance is all too apparent.

D: But there has been an upsurge of the feminine voice over the last century: they now vote, petition to receive the same wages for the same jobs men do, understand that their bodies are radically different from their male counterparts, and are finally beginning to receive health care appropriate to their gender.

A: Notwithstanding, the relationship has been polarized for a millennium or more. The male is the norm.

D: Thanks partly to the Judeo-Christian and Islamic heritages. The male God and male leadership consecrated by religious scriptural documentation.

A: And all this concurrent with the rise of reason and science. What can we make of all this? Parallels abound.

D: I can think of a starting point: What is the human? Is it male or female or both? Does that mean respective or irrespective of their differences?

A: **I would like to think the relationship between them is the human. I will let male and female each retain their separate autonomies. Neither, individually, is human. The human emerges as a product of this relationship.**

D: Both male and female are human beings. The question: 'Who is human?' or 'What is the human?' seeks the characteristics of an ideal. Perhaps the phrase we want is 'fully human', a phrase that speaks to degrees of being human.

A: But again, neither sex can be fully human, since the male and female differ essentially. Unless each is both male and female in some as yet undecided way.

D: Suppose, for the moment, we go back to our dialogue concerning consciousness and self-consciousness. We are convinced that the relationship we created is archetypical of the human mental process. The process is one in which two holistic and autonomous processes, consciousness and self-consciousness, are finally defined by the reciprocity of their relationship. Can't we compare the male and female to these two modes of mental activity?

A: Why not? Consciousness forms relational wholes out of feelings and emotions. It is emotional and intuitive. It intuitionally creates new significance by serially interrelating old and new sensation. This sounds feminine in a general way. Consciousness is temporal, relational, emotional and feminine. But consciousness has no language. Problem.

D: And self-consciousness in the contemporary world is rational, ego-centered, directorial, and therefore consumed by the love of power. And it is the arena of all language. It can welcome the interruptions that consciousness constantly contributes or it can ignore and dismiss these in order to maximize rational control. In the male contemporary world, this rationality is dissecting, analytic, and spatial, breaking down the world into static parts. This all seems very male, but I have to point out that consciousness contributes a great deal to language, such that men may dominate language but they don't own it exclusively. They have the power over language and use it to destroy the dialogue. Without the dialogue, everyone loses.

A: So when we focused on the contemporary inequality between consciousness and self-consciousness, we discovered that this inequality had broken down the dialogue between them in a way that was detrimental to both. The two processes had become as much mutually exclusive as interactive.

D: And we found two causes for that which we deemed teleological. The historical long view showed us that reason, the second child of the mind, had to mature and gain its ascendancy, denigrating emotion along the way. The second was that the more reason tried to absolutize itself and denigrate emotion, the brighter the spotlight shone on the enigma of the senses, since, in the last analysis, emotion can not be subsumed or controlled by reason.

A: So if male and female parallel reason and emotion, the first thing to note is that the autonomy of each gender is assured. Each gender is distinct and will not dissolve into the other. If male and female parallel self-consciousness and consciousness, the contemporary problems of the one more or less apply to the other. The arena of language seems to be an anomaly in the comparison.

D: That leaves the nature of their interaction at issue. Can we use the self-consciousness/consciousness construct to create a different understanding of the male/female relationship?

A: I not only think we can do this, I want to say that the male/female relationship is that very same dialogue between self-consciousness and consciousness externalized as different gender in different bodies.

D: You are claiming that male/ female is an explicit model of the internal workings of the mind?

A: I think so. The obvious gender differences serve to continue to force humanity to keep questioning the internal structure of the mind. I suspect the parallel is anything but superficial. What is roughly explicit in gender is implicit in the human mind.

D: All right. After noting that consciousness and self-consciousness had separate autonomy one from the other, we found that they were most profoundly defined by their relationship to each other. And that relationship we termed their dialogue.

A: Yes, such that neither of these two arenas was able to address human existence by itself. Consciousness discovers the new and important, producing new intuitions and creating new awareness, but it has very limited potential to address the world with its product. Product is the result of rational linguistic manipulations.

D: Consciousness needs the dissecting power of reason to break down that significance into empirically utile constructs. Yet without new creations to analyze, reason is sterile.

A: Just as a man and a woman together produce a child. I think our analogy travels far beyond this reference to sexual union.

D: I agree. As with the mind, unless the two halves are fully inter-operative, the product of our society is less than it could be.

A: In that case, we can expect in the coming years for the pendulum to swing back. We will see a revaluing of the emotional and the intuitive. And women will be valued for their predominantly emotional, relational, and intuitive understanding. This evolution is historical and behavioral rather than genetic. Genetic differences are merely the starting point of the ongoing dialogue between men and women that defines the human.

D: And societal life should focus less on power, aggression, and control, and more on relational significance and self-expression leading to creativity. What in women was deemed abnormal and weak will come to be seen as a qualitatively different kind of strength.

A: That will change the dominance of rational directorial monologue to an emotional-rational dialogue.

D: Which statement evolves our parallels. We are saying that each person has the male and female characteristics within them, irrespective of their actual gender.

A: Yes. The historical inclination toward reason for men and toward emotion for women is the acknowledged starting point. Male and female must each find the balance between reason and emotion. Each must find the balance between self-consciousness and consciousness in their mental processing.

D: Wouldn't there be an innate potential for male-female dialogue to be more creatively productive than male/male or female/female dialogue?

A: In the same way that we deem the mind most effective as a dialogue between consciousness and self-consciousness. Same sex dialogue more often than not produces sterility and agreement, but this is not necessarily so. But heterosexual dialogue is a dialogue that mirrors the autonomous halves of our two cognitive systems. The union is very fertile in all senses of the word.

D: Does a male/female relationship reach equilibrium any more than a conscious/self-conscious relationship does?

A: I do not believe the male/female activity is entropic. We don't want that image. I suspect that, as with the internal dialogue, the male/female relationship has an infinitely expanding reciprocity and growth. I am speaking of an individual couple, but this would be true of society as a whole.

D: Agreed. The ideal is not just balance but balanced reciprocity that becomes ever more creative and productive.

A: Women historically listen better, presence better, relate better, and locate emotion better, but where is their voice?

D: **If the self-conscious 'I' is dominated by reason, it all but shuts down the offerings of consciousness. This is male ego overriding female attempts to dialogue.** Once women move past the passivity created by the male ego, they will find their voice and enact their creativity. Ego is not a master ideally; its true function is to be a transparency between inner dialogue and outer exigencies. Male self-consciousness must become dialogic.

A: Men must learn to listen and feel. Historically men have been the creators, since they effectively repressed women's inclinations, but that creativity is in its infancy. If you strive for creativity and denigrate emotion, what gets through as a creative act is minimal. Our society bears witness to this. When men and women together create, when self-consciousness and consciousness together dialogue, what wonders will appear on the horizon?

D: I think we can bring together the comparisons we have been constructing. I want to summarize the negative current situation brought on by male rational dominance, then move to the center of what these relationships really stand for.

A: Agreed. As it stands, with the self-conscious male ego dominating the mind, we are left with a rational monologue. The intrusions from the female consciousness will be rejected by the ego. Creativity will suffer. There will be little or no dialogue with consciousness or with women. The dialogue within self-consciousness, that all-important linguistic dialogue between 'I' and 'Me', will be treated as a Master/Slave relation and the ego will persist in the rational monologue.

D: Women do talk a great deal. From your remarks I take it that the male ego will converse with the woman but not dialogue, since she is inferior or abnormal. In the same sense he will turn down all invitations from consciousness.

A: In the same way the male ego refuses to dialogue within its own self-conscious linguistic internal conversation. We have created a radical stereotype on male/female relations, and I am sure that many such relations are a great deal better. But our caricature leaves a bad taste. I need to understand the power of the male/female relationship as regards our mental processes. I need to see if it supports the road we are traveling or is simply a hindrance.

D: The most intimate moment of male/female dialogue is sexual intercourse. In it emotional consciousness holds full sway. Here both male and female are dominated by sensation. This act can and is often undertaken aggressively, in anger, and as a Master/Slave relation. But the act itself is massively corrective in its emotional intimacy.

A: Yes, when it is undertaken in love. As a love dialogue, where sexuality listens and responds, self-conscious ego is repressed towards dialogue. This very tangible human model then stands as corrective to all male/female relations. The emotional presencing in dialogic sexual intercourse is powerful, creative, and significant. At orgasm each partner's 'I' disappears and the emotional consciousness of each is fully present. Ecstasy, 'standing outside oneself', refers to this dissolution of the 'I'. Orgasm absolutizes the autonomy of each consciousness by achieving total mutuality of dialogic interaction at all levels. Each partner is at once totally himself or herself because each is totally a part of the other. This passing through the mirror to become one's own reflection is at once the most common and the most powerful model for the fully human. It is a reference point for the personal relationship between men and women, a dialogic reference point both for the dialogue between consciousness and self-consciousness and between men and women. It points, again and again, by its very unique kind of activity, to the potential for the human.

D: Do we then have a chicken-egg problem manifesting itself? Is the consciousness/self-consciousness dialogic intercourse the model for sexual intercourse, or is sexual intercourse, as the primary locus of the discovery of the true meaning of dialogue, the model for self-relationship and the human?

A: Sexual intercourse continually makes explicit what our implicit mental processes are capable of. All the processes we have looked at are ideally a dialogue. I believe, once again, that we do not have a dominance or priority problem. What we have is a very significant dialogue between male/female relations and our internal mental processes. It is not sexual intercourse alone that leads to the human any more so than our mental dialogue alone leads to the fully active mind. It is the dialogue between gender and mental process that most reveals the potential value of each.

D: Once again, the interactivity defines the parts. Past assuring the survival of the species, our sexuality is a compelling model for our own mental interactivity in dialogue. It guarantees that, sooner or later, we will dialogue.

A: And vice-versa. It is easy to become lost in the machinations of our cognition. Sexual dialogic intercourse, what we properly term the 'act of love', has a graphic particularity that reverberates through us and centers us on the nature of dialogue. The dialogue we use to make love is the same dialogue taking place between reason and emotion, and finally the same dialogue taking place between consciousness and self-consciousness. **These dialogues, taken as a group, are the basis of human survival.**

D: Then the most crucial relations in human life all have the same focus: the learning of dialogue.

A: We keep returning to the same place. The human, floating between the man and woman, is their dialogue, whether it is sexual, verbal, or within the reciprocity between the predominantly female consciousness and the predominantly male self-consciousness.

D: One aspect of this talk still bothers me. If male ego does not listen, the female voice cannot be heard. If male self-consciousness does not listen to its predominantly feminine consciousness, there is little or no creativity. Men control language and language is mostly rational. I know this balance could be otherwise, as our theories see this taking place over the next century or two, but *if* there is to be true dialogue, consciousness and women must find their voice. The contemporary world is still defined by power struggles rather than dialogue.

A: The very minute you concede that power is dominant over dialogue, you have reverted to the very world you wish to see changed. I must continue to assert that love, which is the basis of all dialogue, will always outlast the power struggle of male dominance. I have great faith that feminism as it grows and flourishes will bring this message home, not by out-competing the male, but by creating more and more significant dialogue. This whole dialogic revolution will take place in language, where emotional creativity will eventually balance reason.

D: I take heart from your remarks. I forgot to dance. Socrates would be ashamed of me.

A: No, he would only engage you in more dialogue.

D: We end on the same page anyway. The gender revolution can be effectively called the dialogic revolution.

A: Is it apparent that our minds themselves have a male/female component in consciousness and self-consciousness?

D: As apparent as that the dialogue within self-consciousness is male /female in many ways. Power vs. dialogue. The plural dialogic self vs. the monologic ego. All things have their place and value. Balance is all. All dialogue, that is.

A: I am going to put this thinking on the back burner overnight and see what shows up in the morning.

D: Me, too. Get some rest. Make love. Sleep. Focus the dialogue. Tomorrow is the future.

~ CHAPTER VIII ~

SIDE ROADS TO FUTURE HIGHWAYS

Anno: I'm tired of focused dialogue. I know we are supposed to dialogue the future, but let's take a directionless journey.

Domini: To wander is to Boogie. We don't need focus. I was just thinking. By our understanding, wisdom in a human being is the result of countless dialogues. It's the cumulative sense of how to move in relation to other human beings as well as oneself. It's not knowledge but the sophisticated ability to swim in and out of life.

A: Do you think dialogue can be taught? As human beings, we already have several ongoing dialogues in our minds. Socrates taught dialogue.

D: I'm not sure Socrates taught dialogue. He dialogued. You learn by dialoguing. I think it's basically attitudinal.

A: Can't you teach attitude?

D: By example?

A: I see. Like Socrates, by example or not at all. At least you can manifest and defuse those assumptions that are self-injurious and that prevent dialogue.

D: You cannot create another person. You can only try to dialogue with that person.

A: I just realized what the ethics of dialogue are really all about. The ideal is to become continuously creative. A continuously creative human being is living art.

D: To learn how to find beauty and become beautiful. To become an art work in progress. I am not sure that is the human ideal. Like it or not, it is the path we are on.

A: That's what I meant. I think dialogue can be learned. If I try to find the beauty in the other person, eventually I will hear it.

D: If you listen hard enough and they are able to issue an invitation.

A: Experiences issue invitations. Do you think people issue invitations? Do they know that?

D: Certainly. Invitations from people outnumber all other kinds. They can dialogue with you.

A: Are seeing and hearing opposed here? We always speak of listening.

D: I think seeing and hearing are both metaphoric. "I see your point" is not so far from "I heard you".

But there is a difference in orientation. Extremely visual people usually employ their minds more statically and rationally. Oral people are closer to dialogue and what dialogue means, that special "speaking beyond the words". Either group can dialogue if they see the world in motion. It's complex and individual. Language, that is.

A: You don't think language has a specific unit of meaning, such as the sentence, paragraph, or the context as a whole?

D: Only from a rational perspective. Looking at the whole spectrum of language usage, rational language usage must be specific and linear, but in most other kinds of communication I think we convey and receive meaning in spite of the language structure rather than because of it. My understanding is more poetic here. To be confined to syntactic rules is like having a rigid protocol for dialogue. It doesn't work. When you need to fracture syntax to get something said, you do it.

A: And again, there is the value of slang. Breaking through the structure of language to say something that language hasn't said yet.

D: Unless you function better using formal diction. Shakespeare didn't seem to have any trouble. Language is an orchestra with many instruments. Every person picks his or her own assembly of sounds.

A: So all dialogue is idiosyncratic with respect to each person involved. Everybody puts their own spin on the words they use. Everybody's connotative associations are different. Dialogue is communication, regardless of language structure. It's not about the logic of what's said; it's about the emotional meaning tossed back and forth. You say one thing. I hear something else. I speak and a third reference appears.

D: I see that. Dialogic communication is anything but linear. Dialogue has to focus on the quality of movement in speech. One actually tries to hear the music, to find the essential currents in the flow of speech.

A: Which focuses us back on the priority of motion. How hard that is for the emotionally challenged! E movere—to move out. Listen to it MOVE!

D: That takes me back to the beginning of our dialogues. Dialogue doesn't sing or paint or march—-it dances.

A: I remember. I like it. But why "dances"?

D: Singing is monologic and can be melodic. Dancing is all rhythm. My legs dance—and dialogue—with each other. My legs constitute a fast form of listening and responding. There is an irreducible two-ness in dancing.

A: So dancing is leg dialogue.

D: Not just legs. We humans are bilaterally symmetrical. Dancing signifies leg-to-leg, hand-to-hand, arm-to-arm, ear-to-ear, and, ultimately, self-to-self dialogue.

A: Not reducible to a single motion?

D: Never. Back and forth, listen and respond. Dialogue is talk *dancing*.

A: And from talk dancing emerges the creative journey and intuition. All that from a lot of sense data in motion.

D: Which reminds me. I'm tired of this phrase "sense data".

A: Absolutely. We can't be stuck with that. It's bad thinking by our understanding. What is this notion of each sense reporting to its own separate data box? Senses are definitely felt and therefore move. One may be dominant at any given time, but they are all moving and acting in concert. Hey, 'concert'. How about…

D: Don't distract me. Let's use the formal word. If all sense reception is kinesthetic, then what the senses try to apprehend are patterns of motion that are significant or interesting.

A: I don't like the word 'pattern' there. It re-establishes the visual and spatial as dominant. Let me try it another way. If I turn to music, I would describe sense data as significant clusters of sound.

D: The idea you are after is rhythm. 'Cluster' is spatial. Sound applies to only one sense. How about 'coherent rhythms'? Sound patterns are rhythms.

A: That flies. The senses apprehend coherent rhythms in their environment.

D: Sort of sounds like 'wave mechanics'.

A: Conceptualization focuses more and more on motion. What draws our modern attention more and more is the way something moves, or the coherent movement among a series of things moving. The dominant movement might be seen, but could just as well be heard or touched.

D: The dominant movement tends to mask the other movements taking place at the same time. Yet the others are still there and presenting themselves. It makes me think of the idea of overtones in music.

A: Yes. I hear an 'A' on a flute. It is the dominant vibration my ear receives. But present in the 'A' are overtones of sound, a host of other notes less dominant than the one heard. Our senses are like that. The emotional computer must find the dominant note among all the tones, and then must find the coherent rhythm among the tones in that experience and bring it to our awareness.

D: So goodbye to the notion that the senses work independently of each other. Studying sense reception is a study in coordinating movement, a study in kinetics. How is all this presented to our awareness?

A: I can address that from our dialogues. These coherent rhythms burst into our linguistic awareness as complex emotional event with some part more significant than another. We must then identify what that means, either by continuing to follow events or by defining what we feel.

D: In this sense perception would never be simple, as 'to perceive a chair'.

A: That would be the rational and minimalist version. The emotional system can sort out this complex rhythm non-verbally because it is ca-

165

pable of assessing any number of feelings simultaneously and identify what is taking place.

D: And perhaps discover a new coherent rhythm and point to it.

A: And begin a new intuition.

D: And the journey towards intuition is actually one of watching the nature of this coherent rhythm as it moves through language constructs, watching it move across different terrains, as it were.

A: The terrain being language and emotion.

D: The ultimate terrain being dialogue, where talk dances and produces identifiable coherent rhythms.

A: So dialogue is the place where multisensory kinetics translate into coherent rhythms.

D: Yes. The more this coherent rhythm connotes, the more identifiable it becomes. It has to emerge from its environment of miscellaneous motion and become one distinct motion, one that we can identify or name.

A: Which identification is the significant pause in the ongoing dance, what we called the 'Aha' of intuition.

D: Reinforcing our sense of cognitive motion is very productive. I want to go back and kinetically understand everything I thought I knew.

A: To parallel every rational construct with a kinetic emotional one.

D: Something like that. And I still feel the resistance to doing that, the rational prejudice pushing me to make things stand still.

A: If after all we have discovered we still feel that prejudice, think of how much more powerful that prejudice is for people committed to the dominance of rationality and control.

D: It still feels peculiar. Releasing myself into motion feels natural and joyful, while something else tells me to be careful and stand still.

A: Some of our primitive genes talking.

D: What do you mean?

A: Hunting and being hunted. Standing still, taking flight. Taking flight by standing still.

D: I see. Cognitive motion is satisfying when one is moving out, putting oneself in motion, but when one is passive and hiding, motion betrays us to the hunter.

A: Very much so. Dialogue is not about safety. It is active and moving out. Passivity in dialogue is vulnerability.

D: I think it is another form of the hostage syndrome.

A: Which is?

D: People enter dialogue with a sense that they possess a core self which is static and permanent and not subject to change. They believe dialogue is a way of modifying the self without changing the core.

A: So the core self is safety, the hostage against formidable change. But that precludes real dialogue. It precludes real transformation of self. That is just chatting.

D: Let's formalize it. In dialogue there can be no hostages inside oneself. One must leave behind the self as one knows it, or at least offer the self up for transformation.

A: Which, paradoxically, is the only way to avoid vulnerability.

D: Exactly. No one can burn my house when I go on the road if I take my house with me.

A: Too static, your notion of leaving nothing behind. I would prefer a notion of all offense and no defense.

D: That is a prerequisite for true dialogue, but very rare at the start. I believe that happens when one's involvement becomes so great that defense is forgotten.

A: That is also the result of misconception of the nature of the self. If the core of self is always in motion, there is no need to protect it anyway. There is no 'thing' left to protect.

D: That notion that we are our past and our past knowledge is a very powerful assumption about ourselves.

A: And in the first and last analysis, we have understood that the assumption is wrong.

D: I think Sartre understood that best. Habit is very strong. Many people wish to repeat themselves over and over for a lifetime.

A: Which habit precludes dialogue and growth.

D: I'd personally rather saddle up the great steed of myself and let it have its head. Life is in the journey.

A: "There is a certain magic about a road...."

D: Speaking of which, we have wandered through some interesting places this time.

A: I don't think we were avoiding the future of our understanding. I think it was avoiding us.

D: Think we are ready now?

A: Who knows? Yet... I feel some intuition coming on....

~ CHAPTER IX ~

Drawing Up the Ladder: A New Wind Blows

Anno: I've got a really good intuition. The future of our nation is in its children.

Domini: Some of us heard that a while ago. Glad you finally caught up with it.

A: We decided to dialogue the future of our understanding. My first thoughts were of mind-bending technological changes, computerized psychiatry, and things like that. Then I realized that our material is so accessible to a wide range of people that it doesn't have to trickle down through centuries of understanding to be applied. It can go directly into the schools and into the culture.

D: OK. So the primary future of our thinking is in its effect on education.

A: I also discovered a new way to access creativity.

D: Let me try some of that orange juice you like so much. Maybe it helps ferment the brain.

A: I went to sleep thinking about teaching really badly educated street kids. I did that about fifteen years ago. I couldn't get them off my mind, couldn't get back to our dialogues. They really hated to write. When I woke up I knew why.

D: Why they hated to write?

A: Why I couldn't stop thinking about them. Street kids live in their ears. Sophisticated vocabularies, but can't write worth a damn. They hate the written word. So one day when I had a composition to assign, I told them to do it in dialogue.

D: What's the difference? Written dialogue is a monologue. It's like writing a play.

A: No, it isn't. I came up with some very simple special rules that changed all that. **I told them not to use any narrative. You know, like "Philbert then filled his pipe" kind of stuff. Just the talking. I asked them to keep the dialogue to two speakers. I asked them to begin by having the first speaker say any one thing that was personally interesting to him or her.**

D: And the kids thought you were freaking out.

A: A little. **Then I gave them the Golden Rule. After that first speaker says something interesting, the kid has to become the second speaker and reply to the first speaker. And then he becomes the first speaker again and replies to him and so on.**

D: Didn't they find it difficult? Kids not only hate to write, many of them hate to debate.

A: I didn't tell them to argue. I just told them to keep replying until they were finished. And, yes, I let them decide when they were finished.

D: How did they know what to write about?

A: They didn't 'write' in the way you mean. They just kept talking. There were no topics.

D: C'mon. Tell me.

A: The second or third time we did this I had to limit the length of the papers. These kids got talking to themselves and they didn't know when to stop. They loved it. They could explore their own world on paper and get credit for it.

D: You are a sneaky fellow. This written dialogue is a way to train students to expand and refine the creative dialogue already taking place in their minds. You got them listening to themselves!

A: Very much so. It is a wonderful tool to create self-relationship because the dialogic habit eventually moves into the mind and into your interior mental speech.

D: Not so crazy after all. If the kids become good at it, they will come to know themselves a lot better. They will get past a lot of those assumptions they had made about how they were supposed to relate to themselves.

A: They learned to get interested in what they were talking about enough to stop posturing on paper and really get into whatever they were talking about. Secondarily, their relationships to their dialogue partners improved. And the way you treat your partner in dialogue is going to redound on the way you treat your self, classmates and friends. I see no down side.

D: And they don't have the normal resistance to writing you see in schools?

A: I think what schools normally call a 'composition' or 'research paper' is good training in linear analytic thought. It also teaches syntax and vocabulary. All this is absolutely necessary in today's world. But that is all they are taught. And look at who is being taught: pre-and post-adolescent kids who are a sea of swirling emotions. Add dialogue composition to their regimen and they get to explore themselves non-linearly.

D: So the dialogue is basically self-exploratory.

A: Years of that training would make superficial kids profound.

D: At least in their ability to articulate their thinking both aloud and in their own interior dialogue.

A: So this harmless method produces huge results. The dialogues may even lead them to their own creativity and help them be at home with it.

D: And as they get older they can use some of the more sophisticated tricks we have discussed, like suppressing self-conscious language or learning to ride emotion.

A: Yes, that comes later, but who knows? They may not even need it. **The dialogic component of their education would create the necessary balance between the rational and the emotional. I would project that kids would keep dialogue diaries.** That would probably cut down on teen-age psychiatric problems a good bit. There is a world of difference between putting down your thoughts on paper and writing to yourself in dialogue.

D: It would actually give those students a chance to speak to those internalized commands, probably parental in origin, that speak to them all the time. They would begin to see commands as negotiable assumptions. They move from the parent's "Why are you always so negative?" to the internalized "I really am a negative person" to the dialogic "I wonder if I just assumed I was negative". This gradually gives them control of the voices they think they hear.

A: Which allows them to find their own voice in dialogue, and realize that any assumptions they make about themselves can be talked and questioned in dialogue. Their dialogue partner is their closest "friend".

D: Does it become competitive? Or nasty? Or boring? That would be a shame.

A: Students use all these attitudes when they start dialoguing, but gradually plain interest and friendship prevail. It's the beginning of the creation of a true self.

D: So this is a formidable psychiatric and creative tool to introduce educationally. **Do the dialogue characters matter?**

A: **Role playing is useful and a diversion, but you cut down on the effectiveness of the dialogue if the characters in it are predetermined. The young person is not writing a play. She is writing herself. It is better to pick a pair of names that have little or no meaning.**

D: So we introduce a major curriculum change in schools at the middle and secondary levels, perhaps including it in college curriculums. **Over time, students will devote equal time to listening, dialoguing and creating on the one hand and learning analytic reason on the other.** They will begin to shift the rational dominance in our world toward a balance between the emotional and the rational. At the most intimate levels of mental processing, students will develop a respect for the efficacy and sophistication of the emotional computer that they will have found in dialogue.

A: And this would certainly change gender relationships. It would validate the emotional voice that women have tried so hard to argue for in all the years of the feminist movement. And it would make the normally aggressive and apodictic male teenager achieve an emotional balance within himself. My experience with students of both sexes is that the male student embraces dialogue enthusiastically and blindly with the result that its effect on him is more profound. Young ladies warm to it immediately because it is emotional and linguistic, and usually have better foreknowledge of why they are being asked to dialogue. Feminine intuition, you know.

D: And, of course, the often superficial sexual relationships achieve a more human dimension. To whit: young men and young women would have a pronounced inclination to talk with each other as human beings and less as sexual targets. All this from curriculum dialogue: A nation of young Socrateses and Socratinas linguistically creating their relationships!

A: How nice. The USA could really boogie.

D: I want to shift gears and look at the future of philosophy particularly as it affects the society as a whole, but I must first go back to a remark you made. You said: "I've also discovered a new way to access creativity". I have been patient, but you owe me. Were you referring to written dialogue?

A: That's the gist of it but there is more. It should soon become obvious. Go back to the deepest restructuring of our mental processes that we achieved earlier. We found that the relationship between reason and emotion, self-consciousness and consciousness, the linguistic 'I' and 'Me', and the male/ female 'human' were defined primarily by their interactivity with each other rather than the definitions of their semi-autonomous capabilities. What was true of the interactivity in all four instances?

D: Well, that it was a form of dialogue. We widened the understanding of dialogue to include the preverbal and verbal relationship between consciousness and self-consciousness. We also widened the notion of dialogue to include the 'I' and the 'Me' by creating the notion of the plural self. As such, we moved from the concept of the directorial Ego to a realization of the internal linguistic dialogue which actually describes the self-relationship between these internal partners.

A: So we discovered that the motion of dialogue dominates our mental processes. But our dialogues began with a slightly different emphasis. We first had to understand the sophistication of the emotional process end-to-end. And we established a goal for that emotional process.

D: Wait! It should have dawned on me. The outworking of the emotional process is intuition. Intuition is the core of creativity and new understanding. I kept thinking about these kids improving their lives by re-conceiving their personal relationships and got side-tracked. **A lot of their written dialogues are going to have creative results.**

A: And not just personally intercreative results and changes in personality. Their dialogues are going to lead wherever consciousness is going to take them. Some of these dialogues they write are going to involve profound intuitions that are applicable to the world they live in. They will have to use their growing rational skills to interpret and understand what they have intuited, but, in effect, their written dialogues are often going to lead them to creative product.

D: **So, along with self-understanding, their dialogues could produce a new math, or an intuition leading to a poem, or a legal ethics that actually applies to men and women equally. The written dialogue is itself a method for creating intentionally!**

A: That was my insight as well. True dialogue within is as much listening to what you said as speaking to what you said. This listening allows consciousness to come forward and intrude what is important into the dialogue. We said all true dialogues involve this journey.

D: So the dialogue will help these youngsters to become intentionally creative. They can use the dialogue for this purpose as well as learning to create self-transformation.

A: Creativity and self-transformation are synonymous in many cases. And you are still focused on young people. What about us?

D: Well, we have been using dialogue to transform mental processing, and have created a brand new understanding. I should say dialogue has used us, I guess.

A: So if you had to describe our methodology, the main tool we used to access our creativity was dialogue, correct?

D: We were *speaking* in dialogue. We are proposing that these young people use *written* dialogue to access their creativity.

A: The difference is that over a period of years these same young people will turn to written dialogue when they wish to create. It will become second nature to them. This is our new access tool: writing dialogue.

D: And what a profound tool it is. While our other tools are sophisticated methodologically, this tool is obviously the most accessible and useful. So we didn't even have to talk. We could have each taken pen and paper and discovered all we have learned by writing a long dialogue.

A: Somebody already did.

D: Who? I've never heard of any of this material. Where did you find it?

A: **Domini, we <u>are</u> a dialogue in someone else's writing.** Don't you get it? **We are someone else's 'I' and 'Me' having a dialogue on paper.**

D: Our reality is simply someone's 'I' and 'Me' talking on paper?

A: That's the way I intuit it.

D: Then we are not real people! We are just part of someone else's method of written dialogue.

A: And you know what? Why would we really care anyway?

D: Because my personal identity is at stake. I am an individual. You are a separate individual.

A: Careful. Careful. Didn't we say that personal identity eventually disappears as dialogue proceeds? That after a while it is hard to tell who is speaking?

D: I guess so. So we achieved this together, or someone else achieved our togetherness. I have learned so much I don't care where it came from.

A: I've had longer to react to this idea. I understand your 'I' rising up in protest. Mine did to.

D: The fact is, though, this dialogue didn't *have* to be written. Socrates just went to the old agora and let it rip with whoever was around. Our talking *could* have been an intentional live dialogue undertaken for the purpose of creating a new understanding of mental process.

A: Sure. Why take ourselves down? And there is still a final way to intentionally create. Say you are alone. Say you want to dialogue. Can you conduct a dialogue inside your head between you and you?

D: I thought we agreed that our self-conscious process was an ongoing dialogue in the first place.

A: We did. But now we have before us the concept of intentional dialogue. We can write one on paper. We can have one between you and me. These are intentional. I and Me do dialogue all the time, but it's willy-nilly. **Suppose I set out to create a mental dialogue within my mind.** Does that differ significantly from writing it on paper?

D: You mean, make a statement, turn around and reply to it, and so on? You would have more trouble going back over what has been said. I take that back. You and I go back over anything we want. Wait a minute! The directorial 'I' has to intend the mental dialogue and keep it running. It cannot also participate and keep the dialogue on task.

A: I wonder. If the directorial 'I' was used only to establish the task, and then to create the first speaking, would it be needed past that point? Dialogue isn't really 'on task' anyway.

D: That is emotionally difficult. The 'I' would disappear into the dialogic process. That's scary.

A: I suspect that with practice it could become another way to access creativity within us. If a generation of these dialoguing students started trying this as adults and got good at it, would you be surprised?

D: I guess not. I would probably prefer dialoguing with you or writing a dialogue, but nothing says that one day people might not be sitting around holding intentional dialogues inside their heads.

A: So we have another potential way to intentionally access our creativity through dialogue. That gives us **suppression of speech, riding emotion, writing dialogue, speaking dialogue, and conducting an intentional dialogue in our heads. All will launch us on the creativity journey.**

D: The future. Currently, we are still polarized between creative dominance and rational dominance.

Mostly we have a rationally dominant population. The future looks more balanced, a population where many people can both reason intentionally and create intentionally.

A: We may not live to see it. To today's adult, the idea of intentional creativity through proven methods is ludicrous. That's why I think dialogic training in the educational system will surface the idea naturally.

D: That bothers me. We have proposed great changes in philosophical understanding. Should they simply be tossed aside? Do we just let history take its course?

A: I hear some intellectual pride seeping into this dialogue. History is going to 'take its course' anyway. I think the deepest levels of thought provide our intellectual leaders with a foundation for what is taking place. Philosophy is a personally expensive effort for those who devote their lives to it. If we are philosophers in dialogue, **it does not befit us to resent having created something extremely complicated whose product can be had by high school kids for nothing.** That is rather the joy of what we are doing.

D: I agree. It was important to see that what we evolved checked out at every level of thought. **While our societal intellectuals think through the implications and argue them, kids on the street can be using these methods. We have found a way to give away diamonds for nothing.** What continues to amaze me is that the whole notion of dialogue is so basic and humble, that it is there embedded in us all our lives, useful and infinitely available. That it wields so much power is overwhelming.

A: So while the adult creators of our generation can employ the sophisticated methods of intentional creativity to improve and teach their art and thought, the real power of creativity in dialogue will be transforming a generation of adolescents. Wave on wave of children who can learn to create. Our greater gift is the simpler gift.

D: I want to go back to the writer of the dialogues. He used written dialogue to create creativity. Doesn't that suggest that the most powerful creative method, however easily accessed, is written dialogue?

A: But what a let-down! The most powerful method for intentional creativity for the whole human race can easily be accessed by an adolescent. I want to prefer the other, more sophisticated methods, but the author stands in my way. I must admit that the simplest is also the best. Millions of adults will eventually access their creativity by sitting down and exploring the wonder of the written dialogue.

D: All well and good, but calling written dialogue "simple" is still bothering me. I don't like paradoxes. If written dialogue is so easily accessible, how come it took so much dialoguing to discover its potential?

A: It's accessible because it emulates the dialogic processes taking place across the whole spectrum of mental activity. We found that out the hard way.

D: That's not quite it. Let's scrutinize written dialogue a little further. Isn't it just conversation? Don't people converse all the time? What makes this special? And, more specifically, what makes it work?

A: I see the problem. It's accessible and it works, but from our talking it is clear that it must be the most complex mental process we possess.

D: That's it. Why does it work? *Specifically.*

A: OK. When Einstein or an eighth grader picks his or her 'interesting remark' to begin the dialogue, where does the remark come from?

183

D: Got it. Interest is interest in significance, something that is personally important. Consciousness intrudes and suggests the content of the initial statement. A journey has begun.

A: **Why is narrative banned?** It gives the dialogue environment.

D: **It also forces the dialoguers to stand outside the speaking and monitor it. This is not a play. To read or write dialogue without narration is to <u>overhear</u> what is said.**

A: OK. Now, when I become the second speaker, why am I not just continuing a "train of thought"? Why isn't it linear, point after point after point?

D: Because the second speaker must respond, not just say whatever comes into his head or simply further the first speaker's thought. He must listen to the first speaker's words and develop what he hears.

A: **But these two dialoguers are the same person. Aren't they just agreeing on what they already know?**

D: **The first speaker makes a remark that contains hundreds of meanings and associations of which he is not aware.**

A: So **the second speaker must expand on something he hears in the first speaker's remark, and that cannot be known ahead of time.** This begins the outgrowing of the initial remark and an intuitive journey has begun. **But when the first speaker responds again, doesn't he just summarize or reiterate what he said the first time?**

D: That isn't our experience. The **first speaker is not responding to his own words. The thought has moved on.** He is responding, after listening thoughtfully, to the second speaker. He will then further expand the first two statements. Most importantly, neither speaker can know what is coming next.

A: Don't we need a working example of this?

D: Our whole dialogue is a working example.

A: But in written dialogue it is the same person speaking to himself every time.

D: That's not true, and that's the key. The only way the 'same person' could do both sides of the dialogue is if the self-conscious directorial 'I' monitored and controlled the exchanges. And the first thing that disappears, when the writer must respond to his own remark, is that directorial 'I'.

A: But the 'I' doesn't disappear. I have been speaking from myself, my one self, this whole dialogue.

D: Point taken. Let me be more specific. **My 'I' continues to respond with all its imagination and reasoning.** That's why we find this dialogic flow so easy. **But this 'I' under discussion is not directorial of the whole dialogue and is not analyzing and organizing the journey. That journey of expanding significance has its own path. It has a "mind of its own" which we have learned to call "consciousness"**, and travels by its own rule of expanding significance.

A: I have been aware of that fact. The focus is to see where the dialogue goes, not to control it.

D: They are mutually exclusive. **I can either listen and respond and follow the process or control it towards a predetermined analysis, but not both.**

A: So as I continue responding, the dialogue creates its own path. Looking specifically at these mechanics is helping me, too.

D: That leaves us with the last problem of dialogue mechanics. Where, in actual fact, does the dialogue end up, and why does it end up? We have said that the process ends in an "intuitive self-revealing pause", but this is too abstract. What actually happens? I have to see it.

A: Practically speaking, whether you are Einstein or an eighth grader, you follow the path of the dialogue with growing interest, because it is becoming more significant to you. An imperative begins to take shape: How does this turn out? Where am I going?

D: I see it. You will continue the dialogue until you are overwhelmed with intuition. Or maybe until you are simply satisfied. Or tired. **You are finding satisfaction in the journey and keep going until you have had enough.**

A: **And 'had enough' varies with age, experience, education, attitude, and a host of other things.** What everyone who writes dialogue has in common is the sense of growing interest in the journey and its outcome, and a satisfaction that he is taking the journey.

D: All this journeying and intuition could have happened to anyone unintentionally, couldn't it? Humans don't have to dialogue to create.

A: Sure, but to create when you want to, to begin the search for a new you or a new world and know how to get there, that's powerful. Artists won't need inspiration anymore.

D: And writers won't have blocs. Philosophers and inventors won't need a 'new perspective'. And eighth-graders can begin to discover themselves.

A: So when does the directorial 'I' step in and end the process?

D: The 'I' doesn't end it. When the written dialogue has created a new world, however large or small, the 'I' is then called in to analyze and relate the intuition to the writer's life. The plural self of the dialogue yields to the rational 'I'. It has produced a significance that needs attention. The 'I must then find the truth of this new meaning.

A: I am now satisfied. Our dialogic journey has rearranged the world around me, inside and out, and I have much to think about. I hardly recognize my former self. All I see before me are horizons enticing me toward another journey. I am no longer who I was. I have disappeared into myself.

D: I think we are finally understanding the Socratic Boogie. We are still learning from the great humility of his careful and valuable words. His heritage is the endless small dialogues in every corner of the world where talk dances to every imaginable music. His future is to see the thousands of poets, novelists, painters, sculptors, and psychiatrists taking pen in hand and beginning a new dialogue to discover what they really think and who they really are.

A: Thanks for a wonderful full-tilt boogie.

D: Dancing around the throne of God, weren't we?

~ CHAPTER X ~

For Philosophers Only

Aren't We All?

The material of the previous dialogues should be able to stand on its own. That it was necessary to present the material in dialogue should now be obvious. Although these dialogues are self-referent, they do contain frequent allusions to philosophies past and present, nor could this be avoided. This material was derived from the oldest and most comprehensive of the Western philosophical roots. **The purpose of this chapter is to connect the foregoing dialogues to their origins in Western philosophy.**

There are, of course, many ways to do this, as many ways as there are philosophers who have attempted this task. The tenor of this approach is to assert that Western philosophy has its roots in ontology, the study of Being. Having stated this, it is immediately necessary to add that this chapter, which will follow the course of ontology from the Greeks forward, will not consider ontology per se, but as a dialectic between Being and Non-Being. It is felt that the course of Western philosophy is best understood if one sees that the evolving tree of this philosophy has not one but two great trunks. To whit, this chapter is about the evolution and dynamics of the second great trunk of this tradition, Non-Being. The road traveled intends to show that Non-Being evolved from a minor dialectic offset of Being into a fully-fleshed philosophy in its own right.

Nor does this interpretation involve a denigration of ontology. The assertion is that these two great trunks of philosophy are autonomous each with respect to its own domain, both intrinsically and in their evolution. They have not nor will they ever dissolve one into the other. The assertion of the Dialogues is that there are two modes of cognition in the human mental process which, while acting independently of each other, can only be defined and understood by their interaction. In this book, that interaction is termed 'dialogue', both in the literal and metaphorical senses. The term 'dialogue' is preferred to 'dialectic' because over the last several centuries the members of these traditional and fundamental dialectic pairs have become polarized and adversarial. The evolution of Being and Non-Being considered here must be seen to be a peaceful and natural series of interactions. In this sense they will be referred to historically as in dialogue, which is not and can not be adversarial.

The interest here is in the dynamics of the evolution between Being and Non-Being. Exploring this activity involves keeping track of other subordinate dialectic pairs found everywhere in the history. They are specifically: time/space, quality/quantity, connotation/denotation, emotion/reason, freedom/determinism, motion/stasis, presence/absence, and mind/body. Steady and specific shifts in dominance between these dialectical pairs will provide an analysis as to how philosophy evolved, is evolving, and will evolve.

This history is indebted to Phenomenology in general and the works of Martin Heidegger in particular, but the thinking eventually crosses a line that none of the Phenomenologists dared to cross. In the most classical sense Phenomenology was and is heading toward a philosophy of Non-Being. Looked at this way, one observes that Phenomenology produced numerous efforts to turn Being inside out in order to contain the demands made upon it, demands to include kinds of thinking that have never been a part of ontology. Heidegger's *Being and Time* is a case in point. If it can be shown that classical philosophy labored for two millennia to produce a philosophy of Non-Being, the first priority is obviously to give this philosophy a name. The second priority is to see how this philosophy gets its name.

The correct name of this philosophy is Meontology. It does not replace Ontology; it parallels it and is the second great trunk of the tree of Western philosophy. How these two elaborate approaches to human mental processing are able to coexist is the subject of this chapter. To understand the term 'Meontology', one must turn to the Greek understanding of Being and Non-Being, this place where the evolution formally begins.

The Greeks had two pairs of words to describe Being and Non-Being. The Being that was 'ousia' corresponded to the Non-Being that was 'oukon'. The conceptual understanding of this pair is mathematical, spatial, and rational. Being was all that there is, Non-Being was nothing, the mathematical zero, not anything. This pair is used over time in a fairly formal sense. The second pair, however, is 'on' and 'me on'. 'On' becomes the foundation of ontology. On is Being, all that is.

Although this sense of Being is more experiential, it becomes somewhat spatial and static, becoming equated with mass and thinghood. Being is some thing or all things that are. 'Me on' has had as many definitions as philosophers. It was initially understood simply as not-being, or not-yet-being. There is a certain temporal element in this pair. It is important to look at the other meanings 'me on' has had over the centuries. As not-yet-being, me on was difficult to assess. It has been

191

thought of as latent being, as potential, and as a non-spatial dynamic, in the sense of something energetic and about to be. It is mysterious. It is indeterminate and cannot be specified. It is never the mathematical 'nothing'.

Many times it stood for that which had no form but existed in some way. In this sense me on has evolved an important synonym: freedom. The me on is human freedom in the sense of that which could not be determined. The sense here is indeterminacy, that which cannot be designated as a thing.

Heidegger's term is apt: the "no-thing". So the earliest sense of me on is of something not yet formed, in motion but latent, something both waiting to be but also dynamic in some sense. This term's lack of specification carries something mysterious, even when it is thought of simply as human freedom. And this is how the great discussion began in Greece. Human beings are primarily 'on', Being, a something, but they are also something else, some motion that dialogues with Being. That dialogue involves the me on, the no-thing, a concept obviously hard to specify, such that philosophy has maintained for two thousand years that we are being, a something, and secondarily all those brooding notions that are hard to conceptualize and pin down, this brooding latency the Greeks termed 'me on', 'not-yet-being'.

At this point in the analysis one must agree that the me on seems to be a catchall term for what philosophy could not identify or reason. There is 'on', Being, all that is, and the me on, whatever else there is. The me-on appears to be a conceptual safety net to include anything that could not be formulated. And in most instances, even to this day, that has been its function: a negation and reference to what we do not know. The most formidable question then becomes: What arenas of human existence did the me-on protect? What concepts remain latent and unexamined?

From the Greeks to the present day philosophy is primarily about the evolution of reason. For our purposes, reason signifies two things. It is the major tool that connected mankind irrevocably to the empirical world around him. It created all the links we now term technology and science. It operates through analysis. It dissects wholes into parts and reassembles them. It is static and spatial. Secondly, it formed and specified the idea of the singular ego or 'I', the static vantage point from which the world may then be put in order. As such it coordinates motion as a function of things, i.e. it predicates motion as a property of objects. It creates the most powerful of all constructs based on this predication of motion: the subject-predicate language structure.

The primary utility of Meontology is in the way it functions to protect the significance of unidentifiable a-rational cognitive motion. The motion signified here refers to motion as cognitively experienced within the mind. The significant aspects of human activity which Meontology protects are qualitatively diverse and come together only now. What they all have in common is that they are felt to move in an a-rational manner and thus cannot be addressed directly by ontological reason. This point cannot be emphasized enough. These 'motions' are always included by name in rational philosophies but are never dealt with in any depth. One must now name these. Certainly intuition is at the forefront of these. Emotion, long designated by rational philosophy as primitive, is another. Freedom is quintessentially one of these cognates. Art and creativity belong to this mental process. And certainly, at least from the Greeks through the Middle Ages, the most powerful of these a-rational cognates was Christianity, the revealed religion.

As far as our dialectical pairs are concerned, temporality, quality, connotation, the subject 'I', emotion, motion, and presence remained subordinate within their dialectical pairings. Subordinate but by no means dismissed. Meontology carries these notions latently. Their rise to a coherence in their own right is not historically viable yet. Cognitive motion, what all these cognates have in common, could not be systematized and achieve its identity as Meontology. This is due partly to the a-rational sophistication of this kind of mental processing, but mostly to the necessary and powerful upsurge of the rational mind.

What must be performed now is a rather selective look at the history of philosophy considered as a dialogue between emotional Meontology and rational Ontology. The specifics of this dynamic can be argued ad infinitum. One does well to remember that this is an overview in which the interest is primarily in the shifts in dominance between the major dialectical pairs. These shifts in dominance signify two things in our dynamic. First, that rational philosophy, all too aware of what it does not deal with, tries to subsume a-rational areas of understanding such as emotion into its conceptualization. As of the present day it should be apparent that this effort cannot be successful. Secondly, as Heidegger so ably notes, the increasing rational attention given to these a-rational cognates serves to emphasize their significance. More and more light is thrown on the a-rational darkness of these moving, latent, enigmatic aspects of human cognition. What exactly is intuition? Creativity? Emotion? It should become evident that neither rationality nor Ontology can claim these cognates, which pushes one to the proposition that all these elements of cognitive motion cohere in a basic understanding such as Meontology. With this in mind we turn to philosophic history.

With the Platonic and Aristotelian dialectic in place and the initial rise of Christian theism, the stage is set. The likes of Plotinus and Augustine lean toward the meontological elements, but rationalism continues to grow and refine itself. Aquinas is perhaps the best statement of the medieval balance. There are those things which are accessible to reason, including even proofs of God's existence. These are offset by the rationally inaccessible revelations of Christian theism. Deadlock. Looking for a moment at the medieval understanding of intuition helps to see how the meontological latency is carried in an increasingly rational theism. The Platonic definition survives in the definition of intuition as a "Clear and certain percept". Translating, intuition is a kind of self-convicting truth experienced as illumination or a certain light of the mind. It is an important avenue to understanding, but it is not rational. As such, intuition must be emotional, but this is an era when emotion is considered brutal and primitive, such that the place of intuition with respect to knowledge is left undetermined.

This mindset carries through the Middle Ages and arrives more or less intact in the rational philosophy of Descartes. Descartes, too, deems that knowledge originates in the primitive world of the senses. Descartes, too, accepts the medieval definition of intuition as a "clear and certain percept". Descartes' importance along the meontological road is not in the residual Platonic elements he retains but in the subject/object dominance shift he performs. With the Cogito Ergo Sum, Descartes shifts the dominance in knowledge construct formation from the known to the knower. Descartes' insistence that the purpose of the mind is to become totally rational is fitting in light of his pronounced mind/body dualism. The rational mind may well use the sensory, but is, itself, non-sensory. Descartes' helpful shift from the object to the subject is more than offset by the mind/body dualism.

One is left with a picture of a theistic rationality of mind imprisoned in a primitive sensual body. Secondarily, it should be noted that theism continues to exert its influence even in this most rational of philosophies. This remains true even in the philosophy of Immanuel Kant.

Kant's *Critique of Pure Reason* brings rationality to a superb climax, but the meontological elements surprisingly continue to create dominance shifts toward the emotional. Kant, like Descartes, locates the act of knowledge in the subjective 'I'. Kant attempts to subsume Hume's thought into his *Critique*, but the result is that Kant undermines the objectivity of human knowledge. There is here another dominance shift. By asserting that space and time are the filters for all human knowing, and that these are a priori concepts not derived from human experience, Kant confines human knowledge to what he terms the phenomenal realm: one cannot know objective reality, the noumenal, except in the case of three a priori concepts devoid of actual conceptual content. These are God, freedom, and immortality.

For our purposes let us purposely misconstrue Kant's intention. Kant has shifted human reality to the subjective sphere. He has postulated an ultra-real noumenal world whose elements are primarily a-rational and meontological. Kant does bring rationality to a new ascendancy in philosophy, but at what cost? The most interior of the filters used by the human mind is time, is temporal. Any careful reading will show that from this point on time begins to dominate the space/time dialectic , which is an important meontological dominance shift. Secondly, although Kant confined the knowable noumenal realm to God, freedom, and immortality, this assertion does not have the rational rigor of the Critique. Philosophers after Kant are almost invited to speculate as to whether this noumenal realm might contain other important a-rational concepts, a speculation Kant in no way intended.

The particular meontological interest here is that freedom, that latent indeterminacy referring directly back to the root meanings of the me on, has been given an exalted place and separated from reason. In passing, one does well to note that the denigration of the sensory and the emotional as a source of knowledge continues. The rational prejudice is still in place. So, too, does Kant in his *Aesthetics* try to force the recognition of the beautiful toward a more rational construct. One would expect this effort from Kant. In conclusion, the thinker who perhaps more than any other purified the concept of reason simultaneously brought meontological elements such as time and freedom to the forefront of his thought. Kant is an example of the Heideggerian notion cited earlier: to the extent that reason progresses toward its ascendancy over knowledge, to the same extent are a-rational meontological elements within philosophy illuminated and underscored.

Hegel creates the final great theism and the final great metaphysics. Elements of his thinking have been addressed in the dialogues in that his thinking serves as a crossroads and entry point into the beginnings of Phenomemology. Hegel, more than most of his successors, is very modern in his infatuation with temporality and motion. The thrust of this analysis of Hegel runs counter to the way Hegel is currently understood, which should be noted at the outset.

The dominance shifts toward the meontological are overt. Hegel moves from the term 'mind', with all its spatial overtones, to the consciousness/self-consciousness construct, a far more sophisticated and temporal dialectic. Hegel's use of phrases such as "bud-blossom-fruit" and "past-present-future" describing the flow of his logic immediately denotes that a temporal epistemology will be employed. The three terms of this epistemology will be cognitive motions, which is to say that the quality of motion in this trithetic movement will determine its logical conclusions. Dominance shifts from space to time, stasis to motion, and quantity to quality are self-evident. That these shifts are not peripheral to the philosophy but comprise the foundation of it creates an immediate paradox within Hegel's thought. Hegel wants rational control of cognitive motion, which is inherently a-rational, but he believed he would be successful if he used temporality as his epistemological framework.

There is only one viable understanding of Hegel's efforts. He believed that he could take formidable meontological cognates and create a rational philosophy around them. The so-called 'Secret of Hegel', so often noted that it has its own name, is that Hegel attempted to embed an epistemology of intuition within a rational philosophy. This is the equivalent of placing a meontological epistemology inside a rational ontology. The evidence is there. The effort is superb. Let us look at it.

The "Thesis-Antithesis-Synthesis" title of Hegel's epistemology is its most rational description. "Being-becoming-become", which he also employed, is more to the point. The epistemology has three temporal elements which appear to proceed linearly to the third and conclusive one. That is not, in fact, the way they function.

This epistemology is anything but syllogistic. This is not a construction of three statements of which the third is the conclusion. This epistemology involves three qualitatively different temporal motions —past/present/future—which control, by their motion, any content under discussion. There is also a form of temporal atomism at work here. Each of these three temporal movements is itself also comprised of the same three movements. Hegel desired to use the three temporal modes and their interactions as the epistemic framework. For example, 'Being', or 'the past', is becoming present, and will become a future. "Becoming', or 'the present', is present, was a future, and will become a past. Hegel's basic epistemic unit is then seen to be nine-phased: three temporal motions each comprised of three temporal motions. This temporal reciprocity was an attempt to make the structure of the epistemic unit a nine-way interphase which included all compossible interactions between the three time tenses. Stated another way, the epistemic unit describes a complete temporal moment.

The motion of this epistemology is what calls attention to it. These three units are not quantities; they are movements. The third motion, 'become', or 'future', must by its motion create the Synthesis within this logic. The transition from the second to the third movement is critical. How will unity be achieved? And the answer is that, like intuition, it is temporally unpredictable and therefore not rational at all. The second term performs a double negation intrinsic to its motion. It is not what it was—'being' is now 'becoming'—and not what it will be—'becoming' has not yet reached 'become'. And then Hegel enters into this trithetic conceptualization a discussion that indicates without any doubt that he is referring to intuition. If the second term has not entered its transition to the third and unifying movement, it should be "sublated and preserved". The meaning here is subject to many interpretations, but the simplest paraphrase is: 'If the third and unifying motion is not forthcoming, put the second motion on the backburner until the third shows up'. 'Sublated' is literally to 'put under'. Put the second motion in storage and preserve it until the third and unifying motion arrives.

What kind of logic is this? It happens to be the best rational description of intuition that can be given. Hegel is attempting to solve the transcendence problem with an epistemology of intuition. The third and unifying movement—'Synthesis'—represents the intuitive conclusion and the mind's arrival at self-evident new truth. And Hegel did know the most important rational truth about intuition. Even if a thinker describes the three-fold motion of the process correctly, the duration of this process cannot be predicted. That transition from the second to the third temporal movement can take a minute or a year. While one waits, one "sublates and preserves" the process leading into the intuition.

Viewed retrospectively, Hegel knew one more salient feature concerning intuition, and he took full advantage of it. Intuition works off of patterns of sense movement; an important intuition is one that coheres the pattern of any number of sensory movements. Hegel's solution was to repeat his own trilectic pattern over and over in the *Phenomenology*. The thinking here is that if the reader encounters the pattern of the three-fold movement enough times, always across different content, the READER would more than likely intuit that Hegel was writing an epistemology of intuition.

In summary, Hegel comes as close to rationally describing the process of intuition as one can. It is not a rational process. The stakes are high. If transcendence, the acquisition of new knowledge, is intuitional, and one can create an epistemology of intuition, then one has solved the oldest and most formidable of philosophy's problems. At the very least, Hegel focuses philosophy on important meontological elements: qualitative cognitive motion in time, intuition itself, and a logic that is best termed 'series-form' in nature.

Since 'series-form thought' plays a role in the Dialogues, a more specific reference to it should be made here. Each new numerical member of an infinite series reconstitutes not only the immediately preceding member but the description of the series as a whole. The interest in infinite series is the qualitative movement across number; the quantities themselves, qua quantity, are secondary. This is the reason Hegel was described as using 'series-form thought'. The thought form appears linear but it is not. It appears to discuss content, but the interest is wholly in the movement. With each succeeding term, the foundational relationship of all terms must be reconceived. Each qualitative new motion forces one to reconceive the whole pattern of movement involved. One has only to refer to the stream of one's emotional life experience to see the parallel. Each new experience changes the individual, and possibly causes a re-evaluation of whole sequences(or series) of experiences that led up to the current one. Emotional thinking is series-form, and on that score, philosophy owes Hegel a great debt for being the first to verbalize this understanding.

The last comment of interest with respect to Hegel leads one to the future of his philosophy. Hegel was servilely devoted to the use of classical metaphysical terminology. This terminology deals poorly with the language of cognitive motion. And yet cognitive motion is Hegel's central thesis. This writer's conclusion concerning what appears to be a formidable paradox is that linguistic awareness in terms of types of language used is a far more modern concern. In Hegel's day it was not an issue. These comments foreshadow the examination of Phenomenology and particularly Heidegger, where, by contrast, the choice of language all but creates the philosophy.

After Hegel, philosophy splits into numerous branches. The two largest, even today, are Phenomenology and Cognitive Analysis. The latter continues to refine the intricacies of rational thought. Phenomenology, however, begins an inexorable march toward Meontology. Husserl, considered the founder of Phenomenology, brackets off (the 'epoche') human experience from all pre-established knowledge. This recommences philosophy in a new direction, for to deal with human experience as experienced is to deal with emotion.

Husserl, however, for all his innovative ideas concerning the bracketing of the subject -object structure, remains a rationalist. One has only to consider his discussions of temporality: the imagery used is entirely spatial. Current experiences *recede* to the *horizon* of the past. Although Husserl's focus is human experience, he refuses to address cognitive motion as something in and of itself, and so never addresses emotion per se. Put more cleanly, he stands at a distance from phenomena and observes. And again, as did Hegel, he uses the language of classical metaphysics, which inevitably confines one to rationalism.

Not so with Heidegger. Heidegger advances Phenomenology several giant steps toward Meontology. He simply cannot cross the aforementioned line from Ontology to Meontology. In some ways he is too much a classicist. Heidegger's major work, *Being and Time*, is a conceptual and linguistic exercise aimed at escaping ontology while remaining an ontologist. It attempts to turn being into time. Heidegger, the ontologist, wishes to escape the spatiality and stasis of Being, to the extent of terming being the "no-thing", which is after all one of the definitions of the me on. Indeed, at every conceivable turn one watches Heidegger verb-alizing the language, setting it in motion in order to make Being dynamic and temporal. The conclusion, however, remains: Being is being and time is meontological. Both Meontology and Heidegger focus on cognitive motion and emotion, but Heidegger will not go so far as to state that he is no longer thinking from inside reified Being. Again, he will not cross the line.

For all his massive energy and contribution, Heidegger butts his head against many walls, all of them meontological. Heidegger truly does abandon the linguistics of classical metaphysics, and begins to infuse critical terminology with connotative imagery. This effort to combine poetics and philosophy he terms "poetic thinking". Under the guise of performing a hermeneutical task, Heidegger explores the connotations of his terms, expanding the meanings until he finds the one that will inextricably link to the next term. The result is a tightly woven imagistic fabric of thought. This method of expanding the connotations of the terminology runs perpendicular to the entire effort of rationalism to reduce, define, and clarify. Heidegger knows this. His rationale would perhaps be that there is a systematic use of imagery and metaphor which rivals reason in its clarity, but note the differences. Reason is reductive and spatial. Heidegger's language is temporally verb-centered and expansive. Rather than reducing terms to one definition, Heidegger's hermeneutic engages the opposite understanding. Explore the imagistic associations until they interweave and expand into a whole. "Resolution" becomes a form of "anticipation", which together become a form of "care". Each is a major cognate in his work imagistically interwoven with the other.

In Heidegger's later thinking dialogue comes to play a significant part. He might have concluded that dialogue was one of the major roads to intuition, but he did not. He certainly felt that dialogue had some ability to bring things into the light, but his stance was never formalized. Perhaps this is because he felt that intuition was the province of the poet and not the philosopher, even a philosopher who did "poetic thinking". In his essays that discuss poets and poems, particularly the poet Holderlein, Heidegger clearly indicates that the intuition that "unconceals" new truth is the province of the poet, he who "bears the message from the gods". It is after the production of this intuition that the work of philosophy begins. What the poet does is sacrosanct: the philosopher must follow in his footsteps. It is here assumed that Heidegger's highly metaphoric and Socratic dialogues are the closest his views would allow him to come to a combination of aesthetics and ontology. Although dialogue became an important tool in Heidegger's later thinking, he never went on to the next step, which was to create a philosophy of dialogue.

Perhaps Heidegger's most profound contribution is his multifaceted effort to temporalize the language of philosophy. Verb-alizing language and evolving imagery both contribute to this effort. There is an intimate relation between time as experienced and motion as experienced. Heidegger wanted to convey that sense. His most effective language tools in this effort are the widespread use of two pairs of metaphors: "concealment" and "unconcealment" and "presence" and "absence". Nothing conveys the sense of cognitive motion as experienced better than the latter pair. Presencing and absencing constantly displacing each other is a very accurate description of the motion of self-consciousness.

Heidegger's thinking has a certain inconclusive quality. He stops short of stating that cognition is primarily a verb, that human beings are primarily verbs. He stops short of saying that there are two distinct mental processes involved in cognition. He liberates Being from its stasis and spatiality but knows that this is not really Being he is writing about. And why couldn't he see that it was Non-Being that gave him the foundation he sought? To state that cognition as experienced is always in motion and that this motion takes place in a temporally moving environment was the road not taken. Reason stopped him. The rationalist stands still and observes from a distance, locating and categorizing what he finds. Heidegger's attempt to reconceive the relation between the rational and the emotional was doomed to be incomplete because he did not understand either that these two modes of mental process are autonomous or that they are not in competition with each other. They exist to serve their own systems of cognition. That much is true, as far as it goes. Their primary utility, however, is for these two cognitive processes, reason and emotion, to serve each other and the unity of mind.

Heidegger is hopefully the last Phenomenologist to try to dissolve one form of cognition into another. As much as he desired to unify experienced cognition into a distinct whole, he was unable to resist placing this body of material into the same classical categorization of concepts constructed around ontology. He thus remains a somewhat rational ontologist who attempts to fit an a-rational meontology into his conceptual schemata. Perhaps this would not have happened if he had more thoroughly addressed the body and repaired once and for all the Cartesian mind/body dualism. Merleau-Ponty's "body-mind" addresses this issue superbly, resulting in a far better sense of the unification of the mind/body experience.

In the last analysis Heidegger took giant steps towards a meontology. Working against the thoroughly embedded subject/object structure of his native tongue by verb-alizing language is an heroic effort. Creating the experienced sense of temporality by verb-alizing language and employing the 'presencing' metaphor are formidable tools. It is only the inconclusiveness of his overview that weakens his contribution. He will be seen historically as a classical ontologist creating meontological methodologies.

There is one more contributor to the meontological trunk of the philosophical tree: Jean-Paul Sartre. Sartre is precisely balanced between ontology and meontology, both categorically and literally. His approach is unfortunately rationalist. He does, however, maintain a strict division between Being and Non-Being(which he terms Nothingness). The core of Sartre's non-being is human freedom. Being controls the foundation and the outworking of Sartre's thought, and this would at first glance seem to be another classical ontology, but embedded in the middle of this ontology is an autonomous negation termed "freedom". His presentation of this 'freedom' is the cleanest conceptual explanation of this concept in philosophy for one very important reason. In the words of the twentieth-century theologian Nicholas Berdjaev, "If freedom is, it cannot be determined by anything but itself". Philosophers, in discussing freedom, have tended to forget this admonition. Sartre did not. Sartre equates freedom with the human experience of the present tense. Each time the endlessly recurring present presents itself, a human being is newly free of his past. His past is *negated*. In Sartre's understanding, the "nihilating upsurge" of the present casts each of us into new arenas of existence in which we must choose.

Sartre did his homework. Freedom simply cannot be under the control of Being or it is not free. This signifies that, for human experience, freedom must originate as something which enters from without. In Sartre's understanding, freedom negates being each time it occurs. This freedom is the central no-thing of his major work, *Being and Nothingness*. Since both Being and freedom are autonomous yet interactive, Sartre is poised between ontology (Being) and Meontology(Nothingness). He cleanly and clearly recognizes the difference between ontological Being and Meontological nothingness. They neither originate each other nor subsume each other: they are wholly interactive as well as independent of each other. Does Sartre see what Heidegger does not? Yes and no. Sartre sees the division clearly, which Heidegger doesn't, but he analyzes it from the safety of rationalistic denotative language, which Heidegger doesn't. Sartre has his lapses, one of which is confusing emotional negativity with meontic negation, but for the most part these are rational lapses.

In Sartre's case, 'rational lapse' does not refer to the balance between ontology and meontology achieved in his thought; the balance is well wrought. The lapse is that reason tells the story of Being. To truly balance philosophical thought, the story must be told from the meontological side, down to and including a meontological description of reason. Sartre parallels Heidegger here. He will not leave the traditional foundation of rational ontology. Is it inconceivable to them that human beings are primarily cognitive motion, the me on, and only secondarily a thing such as Being? Is it inconceivable that such cognitive motion might have its own voice? Certainly not to Heidegger. Both thinkers, though, tell it from the traditional standpoint.

There is a specific reason for insisting that rational ontology cannot tell this story. The realm of meontlogy is cognitive motion as experienced. Reason by its very nature retards and spatializes motion. The insistence here is that one can only speak about this arena of cognitive motion from within it. That is the task of the Dialogues. The task here is to look at the history of philosophy and draw together the disparate elements that can form a meontology. This analysis has now reached a point where these disparate elements can at least be specified and drawn together. The effort of the Dialogues is to show that these disparate elements taken together form a coherent mental process that is methodological and a-rational. But let us now at least bring them together.

The thesis here is that Western philosophy is about to split into two major branches, what we have termed the major trunks of the philosophical tree. Ontology is obviously the better known trunk. Its components are reason, spatiality, quantum, the object, determinism, and, of course, Being. The components of meontology are temporality, quality, sensation/emotion, the experiencing subject, freedom, art, theism, and creativity. Meontology has evolved down to us from its earliest root in the me on, meaning simply 'not-Being'. The me on is neither negative nor rational, but it is negative from the perspective of rational ontology. It is *not* Being. But what is it? And why have innovative philosophers such as Heidegger, Sartre, and Merleau-Ponty failed to recognize this fact?

The disparate elements of the meontological system were almost always understood to be the minor elements in the major dialectical pairs. From the rational perspective they *are* minor. If, as has been maintained here, these elements form a legitimate corpus in their own right, what single factor or concept brings them together? We have repeatedly used the term 'cognitive motion', but what is that? The cognitive motion of temporality, the qualitative motion of our awareness as it experiences and mutates, and the creative and artistic dynamics of the human mental process all have one thing in common: felt sensation or, simply put, emotion. Rational ontology, in its ascendancy, denigrates emotion because emotion cannot be rationally subsumed or integrated. Reason can certainly access emotion in language but it cannot control emotion; it cannot make it rational. This rational prejudice is powerful and still currently in play. What reason cannot control must be primitive and minor.

The fact remains that there are two major mental processes, reason and emotion, each of which has its own autonomy. Add to this the concept that the meontological process does indeed have systematic and methodological elements that cohere it, and one can begin to see the insistence here that there are two major branches in philosophy, the creative and emotional and the rational and analytic. The meeting ground of these two branches is, as Gadamer so ably noted, language.

As soon as one postulates two separate systems of cognition and comprehension, however, terrible questions arise.

The first and most important is that ontology and meontology would represent an obvious dualism. The term 'semi-autonomous' has been used throughout the Dialogues in consideration of this problem. In fine, what is taking place in human cognition is the activity of two separate systems of comprehension, each with its own systematization and coherence, one rational and the other a-rational or sensate, NEITHER of which can function without their interactive dialogue. This point is very specific. The two systems of cognition can be separated and observed, if the interest is in their separate autonomies, but the ultimate meaning and function of these two systems derives solely from their interaction. This interaction was treated in the Dialogues and was itself termed 'dialogue'. The many does become the one. The burden to demonstrate that the interaction between the two systems is conceptually definitive of their essences is the burden of the Dialogues.

The second terrible question concerns the postulation of meontology as a second and separate form of cognition. Why has not Phenomenology recognized this? Both answers here are speculative. The first is that its time had not yet come. The second is that the rational prejudice dominating even Phenomenological thought precludes the acknowledgment of any significant form of coherent cognition except the rational.

The third terrible question is: How can any form of cognition be both a-rational and coherent? The response is: All of human experience as experienced tells us that this can be so. The existential coherence of the human being throughout his daily existence and movements is not in the least dependent on reason. Reason may intermittently direct the organism, but the acts of walking across a room or recognizing someone walking down the street are immensely complex and in no way within rational capabilities. Meontology, then, is the existential system that coordinates our existence all the days and hours that we are not under self-conscious control. And the rationalist replies that this is simply a blind organic neurological response to various stimuli, the intimation being that it is mindless activity. And here we come to the crux of the matter. Neither love, nor creativity, nor religion, nor intuition, nor art is mindless. They represent the human use of an a-rational coherent system of sensation intimately interacting with self-consciousness through language.

One of the most difficult tasks of the Dialogues was to give Meontology a voice, as it is many times pre-verbal in its cognition. It does, however, have its own voice, and that voice has been battled over and denigrated throughout the history of Western thought. Are the voices, then, of ontology and meontology mutually exclusive? To some extent. They each involve elaborate systems of cognition in their own right. Once again, their meeting place is language, regardless of their origins. As such, for our purposes, this linguistic interaction creates their ultimate individual definitions. This dialogue in which these systems meet is the human condition.

One must return again and again to the most formidable question: How can an a-rational system of cognition be coherent? This issue goes to the roots of the rational prejudice. The classical problem of transcendence, the study of how human cognition produces new understanding and knowledge, has been the central problem in Western philosophy since its beginnings. The primitive a-rational system here termed 'Meontology' has as its focal activity the production of intuition. Or creativity, if that term is preferred. The most frustrating of all philosophical historical efforts has been the attempt to define how reason produces new understanding. The simple answer is that reason does not and cannot perform this task. New understanding is arrived at through intuition. This process belongs to the a-rational system. It is then turned over to rational thought to achieve its outworking. To ask the question concerning a-rational coherence is to ask if creativity represents a coherent form of cognition. Is it not now obvious? Of course it does. *How* creativity operates is another question and the subject of the Dialogues. But let the assertion stand. Creativity is the quintessential goal of this a-rational cognition.

If one has endured these a-rational postulations through to this point in the chapter, a significant but very rational protest remains. If meontology represents a coherent form of cognition apart from reason, why has no one ever found a way to control and operate it? Doesn't that prove that this process is anything but coherent or systematic? If creativity is a form of cognition, why can't it be controlled?

The answer is that 'control' here means rational control. Creativity cannot be rationally controlled because it is not rational. One must here hasten to add that although creativity cannot be rationally controlled, creativity understood as a self-consciously intentional process can be ACCESSED. There are methodologies available that allow one to access and intentionally use this form of cognition. One cannot, using these methods, predicate the end product. Creativity is absolutely not a linear process. And if one is actually addressing creativity here, creativity here considered in all its glory as the fount of new knowledge, is it not apparent that the end product of a creative process is something new to cognition? Does not this fact indicate that the product of a creative process could not be rationally predicated or controlled by definition or logic? The point here is the gist of the Dialogues. There are methodologies which can access this form of creative cognition, ones which intentionally engender the process and then watch it take place. Our age seems to lack all the traditional religious heresies, but the previous statement is definitely one of the atheistic spiritual heresies still alive and well. To speak of intentional creativity is a heresy, for it is the contemporary world's most cherished belief that creativity is the last bastion against the reigning monarchy of reason. The judgment that remains to be made, after one has read and digested the Dialogues, is whether self-consciously accessing an a-rational process such as creativity itself constitutes a rational act. The suggestion here is that one should make a careful distinction between self-conscious control and self-conscious rational control.

On a personal note, and in summary, I believe there is a teleological aspect to the emergence of meontology, the a-rational system of cognition. As vituperative as this chapter has been concerning the current existence of rational and scientific prejudices, it is also felt that the historical ascendancy of reason over all other thought forms was a necessary evolution of the human spirit, and an immensely beneficial one at that. The quarrel is with those who would now absolutize reason and make it synonymous with reality. That is the kind of prejudice that would keep one from seeing an entirely separate form of cognition taking place in one's own mind. The contemporary world seems too steeply pitched toward the rational. And the damage is real. Have no reservations about it. The rational ego can inhibit and all but block creative cognition if this ego achieves a certain level of dominance. That is its tendency.

My teleological understanding is not so grand as the Eschaton. It is really quite simple. Now that reason has established its worth beyond any shadow of a doubt, the roads of the future are open to the exploration of the second great form of cognition endemic to the human condition. The time for the exploration of intentional creativity has now come. This exploration will right the balance between reason and emotion within the human condition, both at the individual and the societal level. "Righting the balance' is an historical corrective, but the phrase is also a prelude to a description of the ideal human condition, one in which creativity and reason co-opt our mental process to produce the splendor of our as yet unimaginable future.

Thank you for your patience.

~ CODA ~

STURM UND DANKEN

Whoever composes on the
Surface of the world
Leaves chaos as he found it
And yet

If an afternoon drifts into
A gentle, green little rain,
There is this
Pitapaphony.

Which is not the pouring metered
Lucidity of the central sense,
That silver rain that is Bach,
But a first sounding,
Simple moments
Before a raucous rip of light
Scatters the listening darkness
Forever,
And creates the necessary wound.

As then,
Droplets to drops to
Great drops of bloody sweat,
Rhythms to rhythm,

Rivulets to rills to rivers,
Rushing on to a desperate quest for
The litanies of order,

Chasing up the soul's valleys
After a wet, wet thunder
Ascending,
Toward lucidity with an
Ozone stench,

Toward lucidity and through,
On past the elegance of Bach to outer sky,
Every sense filling its every cup,
He finds himself deep,
Dancing within the dance
Of chaos as he made it,
Lost to his own music.

Until,
After the latest longest pause,
Rivers to rivulets,
Rhythm to rhythms,
Drops to droplets,

Very drop of very drop,
There is this residual
Pitaphony.
The composer: a storm within a storm,
Giving thanks,
Mocking calm.

Printed in the United States
By Bookmasters